Hitting
BLIND

Hitting
BLIND

The New Visual Approach
To Winning Tennis

Dr. Harold Stein
Dr. Bernie Slatt

Musson Book Company
a division of General Publishing Co. Limited,
Don Mills, Ontario

First published in 1981 by
Musson Book Company,
  a division of
General Publishing Co. Limited,
  30 Lesmill Road,
Don Mills, Ontario
M3B 2T6

Canadian Cataloguing in Publication Data

Stein, Harold A., 1929-
  Hitting Blind

Bibliography: p.
ISBN 0-7737-1044-2

1. Tennis. 2. Eye. 3. Vision I. Slatt, Bernard,
1934-   II. Title.

GV995.S73   796.342   C81-094185-6

Except where noted, all photographs are the copyright of Russ Adams, Russ Adams Productions, 49 Bear Hill Road, Reading Massachusetts, U.S.A. and are used with permission.

First printing

ISBN 0-7737-1044-2
Printed and bound in Canada

Dedicated to
Alex, Ronny, and Henry Strasser
for a decade of
exciting Sunday doubles.

B.S.

For my children
Raymond, Laurie, and Gary,
who learned everything I know about tennis
and went on to achieve.

H.S.

Contents

Preface

Why should two middle-aged ophthalmologists, who have never played professional or highly ranked amateur tennis, write a book about tennis — it is definitely not our territory. However, after hearing coaches scream "Keep your eye on the ball until it strikes the racquet," we decided to butt in. Why should a tennis coach teach visual physiology? It is just as absurd as us teaching tennis. The visual responses to this fast-moving game have never been covered in depth. Yet tennis is a visual game. We decided to apply our technical expertise in this area to this sport.

First we thought that it would be necessary to produce strong scientific data. It became important to monitor eye position. If we could show that the eyes do not look at an approaching ball and are not capable of following it into the gut of the racquet, then our thesis would be proved. Now, there are many ways to monitor eye position. But every method we attempted required the head and body to be still. We were stumped. Electronystagmography, laser scans, measuring the deflections of corneal retinal potential could not be applied to tennis. Then we discovered photography. In our daily newspapers it was grossly evident even to a non-professional that the eyes were not on the ball. We looked at pictures of all the major professionals from Borg to Connors, and from Austin to Goolagong, and most of them revealed the same discrepancy. We obtained pictures from magazines, newspapers, and finally from Russ Adams, a tennis photographer of world renown. Most of the pictures were the same. On fast balls, the player never had his eyes on the ball. There were shots taken by independent photographers of major tennis stars in regular tournaments. We were in business with this data. We had proof. We didn't believe it would be so highly visible and apparent.

Then we studied flicker strobe-like sequences to see what happens to the eye when a player receives a hard flat serve. We looked at the visual responses required for the lob, seemingly an easy shot but poorly handled by most players because they did not know how to trace a ball moving in empty space. Could the eye really give accurate information of which ball is in and which is out? The data was fresh and surprising.

That is why two ophthalmic types decided to stick their noses into this exciting game. Luck would have it, we were able to reap the benefits of our sons, one of whom had a long interest in photography (Jordan Slatt), while the other had spent a considerable period of his life as a teaching tennis professional (Raymond Stein).

We were in reasonable shape to write a tennis book. The visual physiology of slow following eye movements and fast eye movements called *saccades* was well documented in the scientific literature. It had never been applied to tennis. Scientifically our position was strong. The photography just gave us the visual evidence that could appeal to anyone's sense of reason.

The results of our investigation were not pursued as an academic exercise. The appreciation of the visual responses in tennis should change current coaching techniques, alter the approach to line disputes, give insight to racquet selection, and alter tennis strategy. It is not a panacea or recipe to cure all tennis ills, but it should help anyone to appreciate and play the fast game of tennis better and, of course, with more pleasure.

Acknowledgments

We would like to thank two individuals who have contributed heavily their time, energy, and effort to the publication of this book. Our sons, Raymond Stein and Jordan Slatt, whose credentials are provided elsewhere in this book, have shared with us the pleasure and pain of research and writing.

We also wish to express our appreciation to Mr. Norman Deer, our senior artist, who has helped us from our first ophthalmic textbook to our present effort. We are also indebted to Mr. Gary Stein, whose tennis talents and artistry have made him an invaluable aid in the design and execution of the diagrams.

We have borrowed some illustrations from our own textbooks, *Fitting Guide for Hard and Soft Contact Lenses,* and the 3rd edition of the *Ophthalmic Assistant,* and we acknowledge the C.V. Mosby Company of St. Louis for permission to use this material.

We were fortunate to have the services of one of the most distinguished, high-profile tennis photographers — Mr. Russ Adams. He has covered all the major tournaments and is widely recognized as a top touring professional in his own right. His pictures are always dramatic, clear, and from our point of view invaluable, because they show the discrepancy between eye gaze and the position of the ball.

Mr. Bernard Gluckstein, a lawyer, tennis buff, and fitness enthusiast, contributed in many ways. He read and edited the book, took many photographs that were used, and conducted interviews with Renee Richards, Howard Head, and other top tennis people. His enthusiasm for the project just made us try a little harder. It was our great luck to have his personality carry us forward.

Finally we would like to thank Susan Stoddard who saw the importance of this tennis book. We are also appreciative of the help of Bill Hanna, and Don Loney for editorial direction.

Raymond M. Stein
Technical Editor
and Consultant

Raymond Stein received a ranking in Tennis in Ontario and Canada throughout his junior years. He was ranked in the top five in Men's Open Tennis in Ontario. He was certified as an instructor by the Canadian Tennis Association. He became a member of the Teaching Tennis Staff at Newcombe's Tennis Ranch, New Brunfelds, Texas, under John Newcombe and Clarence Mabry. Ray Stein organized summer Tennis Clinics 1975, 1976 and 1977 in numerous cities throughout Louisiana, Texas, Oklahoma and New Mexico.

He attended the Wharton School, University of Pennsylvania, where he played on the Varsity Tennis Team in the Ivy League. During his academic years he was designated a Benjamin Franklin Scholar.

After completing his undergraduate years, Ray Stein entered the Faculty of Medicine, University of Toronto, and worked towards his Medical Degree. While at the University of Toronto, he played on the Intercollegiate Tennis Team which won the Ontario Championships.

Jordan L. Slatt
Photographic
Consultant

Jordan Slatt has had intensive training in photography at Ryerson in Toronto, and at the Banff School of Fine Arts. He has worked professionally covering the Mennen Cup in Squash, and the Rothmans Tennis Tournament in Toronto. He has acted as a tennis photographic consultant for York Racquets Club, and other tennis clubs in Toronto.

He has done freelance work for Canadian Newspapers, including the *Sun* and the *Star* of Toronto.

He is bilingual in French and English. He currently is a student at Western University, studying economics. Jordan was responsible for the photographic data obtained from Russ Adams — the noted tennis photographer. He went through thousands of pictures and sequences, selecting the best and analyzing the total into meaningful material. Without these photographic insights, this book could not have been documented.

PART ONE

Visual Clues On Tennis

1 Can You Keep Your Eye On The Ball?

We stress the importance of the visual component in improving one's game of tennis, so we must identify the limits of our visual apparatus. We must also discover how the use of our vision can contribute to an improved tennis game. For example, a player who believes he can follow the ball into the racquet cannot make a great return as the ball is too fast for his eyes to track.

It is true that some people are much quicker and more agile than others and some people have superior vision be it their central vision, their depth perception, or their peripheral vision. Each has an important bearing on one's athletic ability and, just as there are exercises to improve conditioning such as jumping rope and calisthenics, there are also things one can do to improve vision and concentration that can help one identify a tennis ball better. How to gain the maximum benefit from visual clues in order to play winning tennis will be the theme of this book.

How quick is the eye?

Almost everyone, at one time or another, has been to an eye doctor and has had their vision tested. The vision check is done as you sit in a chair and look at a wall or projected eye chart. Your eyes and the chart are quite stationary so this test is for static vision. If you see 20/20 in each eye, it is a triumph of sorts — your eyesight is normal — you can resolve two separated points at a distance of twenty feet. Does that mean you have a superior tennis eye? Not at all. In tennis everything is moving — to construct the same test model, you would have to be running a treadmill, with your gaze constantly moving, trying to locate a fast-moving projectile in space in which the contrast and background is variable.

So there is no relationship between seeing well in the traditional sense and having good athletic vision or dynamic visual acuity. It is possible to have wonderful stationary visual acuity and poor dynamic visual acuity. Midway games in which moving ducks have to be "shot" are handled well by few people. Prizes are given to those people with good dynamic visual acuity — the ability to follow a moving target. It requires judgement, experience, contrast, good normal stationary vision, and proper illumination. Few people develop great dynamic visual skills because these skills are not demanded every day. With reading, writing, or working, the head and eyes are usually still as is the object of regard — the papers or the work bench.

Motion can disturb vision. The man who tries to read his briefs on the subway or the woman who attempts to finish her magazine article on the bus find that motion makes reading difficult. Coping with a serve is also difficult because of the element of motion — the player must react both to the ball and the server which are moving.

How well do you see while you are in motion? No one can tell you. There are no commercial tests to judge the visual thresholds of the eye. In a sense, the eyecare specialists are far behind the cardiologists who employ a variety of moving stress tests to determine the function of the heart. Aerobics have become part of the medical and general jargon. Everyone understands the need to exercise the heart and lungs but because these organs seem to be working well at rest does not mean that they can handle the stress of exercise and increased oxygen demands of a tough five-mile run. Can the eye perform well under moving stress? A tennis athlete may routinely do his exercises but may have inferior dynamic visual acuity. He may constantly see the ball late and make errors in judgement because he cannot cope with the sensory demands of the game.

The truth of the matter is that our visual equipment is

severely limited. Tennis is tough on our eyesight. In baseball, the ball may come in as fast as a return of service, but the batter is standing still in his box. His eyes are directed ahead and the head is still so there is only one moving variable — the ball. In tennis, the eyes, the head, and the body are in motion both horizontally and vertically because as you run you not only move laterally but you move up and down as well.

The eyes make very slow following movements. Move a finger back and forth before your eyes like a pendulum keeping the half moon in view at the base of the nail. Speed up the motion. It doesn't take much speed to blur the image of the half moon. Turn your windshield wipers up to "fast" and see if your eyes can follow them. They may make a few lateral following thrusts and then give up. Or take a pencil and move it back and forth about eighteen inches from a friend's eyes and see how soon his visual tracking movements break down. How effective would the eyes be following the ball off a fast flat serve?

In tennis, our eyes cannot track a ball unless that ball is going extremely slow. One might be able to follow a lob arching up and descending slowly, but even on the ball toss for the serve the eye doesn't follow the upward motion. The eye looks up and then the ball is tossed into the field of vision. The velocity of the ball being tossed up is just too great for the eye to follow its ascent.

For fast tennis, the eye cannot follow the ball because there is no mechanism that allows the eye to make fast following movements *and keep that ball in sharp focus.*

Now the eye *can* make fast movements. They are called *ocular saccades.* These fast movements are used when we watch a parade, read, or try to capture the flight of a high velocity missile like a tennis ball. One might ask, why don't we use our *ocular saccades* or fast eye movements when tracking a tennis ball? It is precisely what we do — unfortunately, when our eyes move quickly, our vision is suppressed.

Actually, it is suppressed to the level of legal blindness. What we do when we read, for instance, is shift our eyes quickly from place to place and we take in information only when the eyes come to rest. It may sound difficult to believe, but you can prove it to yourself. Place the index fingers of each hand up and hold them almost twenty inches apart. Glance quickly from finger to finger in a back and forth motion. Now do it in front of a mirror. You will find that you see each index finger as your eyes come to rest — *but you will not see your own face in the mirror.* You will only see clearly when your eyes are still. So fast eye movements can provide information between two points on the trajectory of a tennis ball, but they cannot give a player information all the way to the racquet because of visual suppression.

In a tennis game, this means that if you have to make a visual correction at the last second, and the eyes must be shifted to a new trajectory, in all probability the stroke will be poor. The slice, for instance, can't be tracked well by the eyes. If it is not anticipated, the ball will be hit on or near the frame of the racquet causing a misdirected return. The change of direction after the bounce can't be discerned well because of the last-minute motion-demands made on the eyes.

How does the eye try to track a fast ball? Consider the return of serve. The type of serve can be expected from the motion of the server because a flat serve, a slice, and a twist look quite different. The ball is struck and, although it cannot be seen clearly, its flight pattern can be estimated with relative ease provided the player does not move as the ball is served. Somewhere near the bounce, the player will lose the ball — the ball enters the zone of fog. The exact point when the ball is lost will depend on how well the court is illuminated (it is better to play a great server during the day than at night), the contrast between the colour of the ball and the colour of the court (fresh balls should be employed for contrast as much as bounce), the dynamic visual acuity of the player (the occasional or slow tennis player will be blinded by speed quite early), and fitness (fatigue causes the player to see the ball late). So near the bounce, the ball approaches the edge of the player's field of vision. He must move his eyes to bring the ball into view and project the ball's probable direction. If the ball hits a pebble, is carried by the wind, or slices in an erratic direction, the chances are the player will make a bad return. His body is in motion in response to where the ball *should* be and his sensory and motor apparatus are not fast enough to make a lightning-quick change.

So consider the best conditions for making a successful return. The ball is coming on straight from a bounce directed from a hard, flat serve and there are no last second variables. The ball is coming directly to the player at a speed he can't follow. What does he do — he makes a series of fast movements of his eyes and picks up a piece of the ball in space just like a reader jerks his eyes, stops, and picks up visual information. If the ball is not going too fast he might make one or two of these fast *saccades* before abandoning the ball altogether.

A perfect return by Harold Solomon. He strokes the ball early and has anticipated well — his eyes are looking in the direction the shot has come from.

If the player is in motion, he doesn't even attempt to make these fast corrective eye movements. His eyes remain in front, glued to the point where the ball was last seen clearly. The photograph of Rosie Casals demonstrates that the eyes invariably make no attempt to follow the ball.

The average player thinks he can see the ball right to the racquet, tries to do so because he has been coached in this way, and fails miserably. The ability to scan a ball in space takes practice, just as speed-reading does. The eyes must be able to take in a great deal of information when, for a millisecond, the eyes freeze fast motion. Frequent and long visual stops are of no use in the fast game.

● Can you keep your eye on the ball?

In tennis it is assumed that, at the very best, everyone can keep their eyes on the ball until the moment that the ball actually strikes the racquet. It seems to be the first lesson of tennis and an adage that is reinforced over and over again as the skills of the player progress. Many of the mistakes in the game are thought to be a reflection of a player's visual wandering and a lack of visual discipline.

We believe that the visual element of tennis is important and should command as much respect as the grip, the racquet swing, and other aspects of the game. It is time that ophthalmology was formally involved with tennis in order to bring a little science to the locker room. It is a little easier for us, as ophthamologists, to bridge this gap than to expect tennis professionals to become students of visual physiology.

At the beginning, it should be stated that the eye cannot follow a flying missile at high speeds. On looking up one can see a Concorde jet moving in the sky at the speed of sound; however, the eye doesn't have to follow the airplane moving along with this great velocity. The flight of the airplane is within the viewer's field of vision. That field of vision is a person's total visual world and encompasses roughly 180° to the sides and 90° above and below the horizontal. To come into view an object must come into our visual field. You can test your own field limits: Bring your hand into view by moving it horizontally and continue to move it until it is out of sight. The expanse of our field of vision is large and everything in it can be seen with relative ease regardless of speed. A high-speed chase scene on a movie screen can be witnessed without so much as a flicker of the eye. The whole episode occurs in our singular field of vision and it is far off.

But what happens when things move out of our visual field? In the case of a jet, it is a simple adjustment — a small movement of the eye changes the scene and now the object of regard has a huge new space to move through. At a distance, the physical size of the visual field is enormous. But when an object gets closer, the reverse happens. The size of the field gets smaller and visual adjustment to keep something in sight speeding toward us is not easy. In effect, whatever is coming close to us comes to the edge of our visual field and we have to move our eyes to keep that object in view. A race begins between the flying object moving toward us and our eyes' ability to keep it in sight. If there is any speed to the ball, puck, birdie, or whatever happens to be moving toward us, the eye will lose the race because the eye can only track an object clearly when the object is moving at a slow speed or a great speed in a large visual field.

All athletes playing visual sports suffer the same visual handicaps. A baseball batter can easily see the ball thrown from third base to second base because the action is in his distance field. But when the pitcher throws the ball directly at him he can see the wind-up, and the ball moving toward him only to a point halfway down the approach. Then his visual guidance mechanism leaves him. If a professional baseball player could see the ball all the way into the bat, the best ones would bat 1.000 and not .333. But baseball, from the standpoint of the batter, is a uniform high-speed game with all balls travelling approximately seventy to one hundred miles per hour.

Tennis is not a uniform game with regard to speed. There are ten-mile-an-hour shots and eighty-mile-an-hour returns of service shots. The velocity of the ball varies with the skill of the player and the type of shot — the serve, volley, and overhead smash being the fastest — and the position at which the ball is intercepted — the closer to the net, the faster the ball. A bounce, on the other hand, slows the ball and the type of court surface affects the bounce, clay surfaces being the slowest and grass the fastest. A tennis player doesn't really develop great visual skills at dealing with speed because he may only hit a fast ball on the return of serve. The first serve is often a bullet and may speed out of bounds. The second serve may have less speed but frequently twice the spin. If a player manages to return the serve then he has two to four ground stroke shots per point and these are at relatively slower speeds. Visually, the techniques for following slow and fast balls are quite different and most players do not make the adjustment to their game predicated on the speed of the ball. In fact, it is a widely held belief that one can and should keep his eye on the ball until impact regardless of the speed of the ball.

⬤ The zone of fog

No one ever sees the ball hit the racquet. Even a slow ball that can be followed almost to impact cannot be clearly defined because of the blurring movement of the racquet. When swung through the air, the racquet appears as a blur — the individual sequences of the racquet's motion cannot be seen. The broad outline of the racquet can be visualized but not the gut or its markings. This is the blur zone or zone of fog.

Rosie Casals plays the ball well in front of the body to reduce the zone of fog. She does not attempt to follow the ball into the racquet.

For all intents and purposes, hitting the ball is a totally blind act. Despite the theory that the ball should be hit in the center of the racquet with the orientation of the racquet to the ball at right angles, it cannot be done. The player never can prove if he did it. There is no eye witness unless his game is recorded by video tapes or high-speed photography.

But why try and exert some control over the zone of fog? If you are told to hit the ball knee-high at the forward edge of your stroke, how do you know you have accomplished this if you can't see the actual impact?

Around the area of impact, there is a zone of fog. This zone becomes denser as the ball increases in speed. This means that when you hit a fast ball there is a longer perimeter of visual loss when the ball is coming to you and as it leaves your racquet. The fog zone is more dense and wide if the player is on the move as opposed to being still. It is enlarged normally

Ilie Nastase makes no effort to follow the ball to the point of impact.

with fatigue and with poor lighting. Good players dislike playing at night because the ball is lost earlier in this zone of fog.

The degree of fog that surrounds impact can vary with the dynamic visual acuity of the player. The dynamic acuity is also quite variable as it depends on fitness, freedom from fatigue, judgement, and the individual capabilities of the players. In random photography shots in which we examined three

Connors makes a fantastic two-handed backhand return on the run. He has no visual control of the ball but concentrates on the point where his opponent made the shot.

thousand action shots of the professionals, there was a profound disparity in the ocular hold on a moving ball. Bjorn Borg seems to have excellent dynamic visual acuity and could track the ball close to the racquet. However, players such as

Jimmy Connors and Vitas Gerulaitus rarely seemed to have their eyes on the ball. Their zone of fog was large and they compensated for it by looking ahead in the direction that the

Connors makes his shot but appears to be gazing directly at the camera and not at the ball.

ball was coming from. Obviously a lack of dynamic visual acuity is not a stumbling block to playing great tennis. Most of the professionals we studied seemed to abandon the ball with their eyes as it approached the fog zone.

Tracking the ball as close as possible to the impact zone is not feasible or desirable for most people and even among professionals — Borg is the exception. It is not productive to track the ball close to the racquet when dealing with a fast ball.

Can this zone of fog be deliberately altered? It is possible to reduce the size of the fog zone but you can never eliminate it. The easiest way to reduce the size of blur or fog zone is to slow the game down. Most players do this. On the first serve, they step back to take the ball at a slower velocity and although they can never see impact — that is, the ball striking the strings of the racquet — they do reduce the zone of fog which means a longer visual hold on the ball. There is a fundamental risk in adopting this strategy. The farther back a player stations himself, the greater is his displacement from a well-placed ball to corners of the court. For visual security, a player gives up command of the court and is forced to run excessively. By running, of course, he defeats the purpose of staying back — visual stability. It is a "Catch 22" of tennis. The player stays back to receive a slower ball and increase his visual tracking of the tennis ball. Unless the ball is hit directly toward him, he must run twice the distance to reach the ball which in turn enlarges the zone of fog again.

Why isn't the average player aware of a fog zone? The average player fills in constantly and thinks that his visual game is complete. A tennis player knows how to get training for his forehand and backhand, but there are no visual training programs in tennis so he assumes that the function of his eyes are perfect — that they serve him well at all times which is not true.

In fact, not only is the sensory side of tennis simplified to "Keep your eye on the ball," there are elements of exaggeration. Some players claim they can see the seams of the ball, or its label, as it travels through space. Some players say they can see the ball at impact as it bends the strings and leaves the racquet. Others boast that their eyes are so fast they can see exactly where a ball bounces even when the ball is going eighty mph and they are running flat out to make a shot. Players claim they can determine the precise point their ball lands in their opponent's court, even at the baseline.

Tennis athletes understand little of the eye's function and are not aware of a remarkable drop in acuity while running. They may not be aware of closing their eyes when confronted with a high, fast shot while playing the net, or the zone of fog because they hit so frequently. It does not matter that the shot is weak, late, or misdirected. The players invariably assume that they did not hit the ball right but do not realize how significant is their inability to see.

There are other instances when a player's game is affected by an unawareness of visual loss. The average person isn't aware that he or she will blink an average of sixteen to twenty times per minute and suffer an intermittent loss of vision. And if we are near-sighted, few of us are aware that our visual world seen through a pair of spectacles is smaller than normal, distorted, and limited in scope.

On the tennis court, it is our brain that adds the clarity when in reality there is none. The brain completes the trajectory of the ball and seems to keep the ball in focus even when we are hitting on the run. The great visual delusion of tennis is that one can see the ball at all times and keep it in focus. The optical illusion is called *completion phenomenon* in which a player believes he sees the ball during its entire flight.

Even the best players are not aware of visual judgements they must make. They play the game properly but have little insight into the role of their eyes and limitation of vision.

● The slow game versus the fast game of tennis

Most tennis beginners are reared on the slow game of tennis. Easy shots are hit to them well within their reach and all they are expected to do is to hit the ball back. Eventually they learn how to stroke the ball and add such things as hitting while on the run and consistently keeping the ball in motion. The running game comes after the stationary game. The player who has been spoonfed balls to center court finds it a different game when he has to run. He has to pace himself, he requires earlier preparation for the shot, and finds he loses a great deal of visual control. Running simply blurs his sight.

With a slow-moving ball the player is visually secure. He can see the ball glide over the net, hear it bounce, and then watch it as it approaches his racquet. He cannot see the impact of the ball against the racquet because the racquet is moving. If the racquet were held still, then the impact could be seen. So with a low, slow ball, the eyes can follow the ball close to the hitting zone where impact takes place. Now if the ball should veer to the right or left after the bounce, the player's eyes could track that ball through its aberrant pathway and his reflexes would respond.

The luxury of slow tennis is time. The eyes can see and the body can afford to move leisurely through space to reach the ball. A full tennis stroke can be made with the arm back in preparation, ready for the smooth stroking motion and a complete follow-through. Playing slow tennis, one soon feels like Bill Tilden or Bjorn Borg.

The fast game of tennis heats up the action. Most of the points in the game are won or lost on speed — return of service, net play, the overhead smash. Speed on the ball constitutes such an advantage that the server in the professional game must win his serve or otherwise face an uphill battle. The emphasis on the serve is high because the tennis player, like the baseball player, misses so frequently on return of service. The professionals may not miss the ball entirely but few can return a serve that is strong, fast, and well placed — that is, an offensive shot. The average player cannot really expect to learn to improve his game until he learns the fast game.

What happens when a slow player meets a fast player? A slow player gets beaten badly because their slow game dynamics do not fit into the fast game. On some shots, the player is unable to cope with speed — the serve is truly a cannonball and he cannot handle it. But tennis is a mixed game so even with better players slow shots at the baseline are still tender morsels available for the hungry slow-game player. These he can hit. He has been trained on slow shots, has an eye for slow shots, and has a stroke that takes time which a slow shot provides. But he can't win — he cannot progress until he learns to cope with speed. He is stuck at the bottom of the tennis ladder.

What is visually different in the fast game? In the fast game, the player doesn't have the advantage of seeing the ball right up to the hitting zone. The faster the ball travels, the earlier he loses it. So on a return of service hit by a powerful server, the ball may be lost from view before the bounce. The sound of the bounce tells the player where the ball is. If a train happens to be going by or there is a great deal of noise in the area of the tennis court, then it is very difficult to play the fast game. The speed of the ball is such that when it hits the edge of the player's visual field, it cannot be followed. The player on the receiving end of such a ball does know one important point — where the ball is coming from. A good player will move in that direction. His eyes are not on the ball, but are looking toward the area from where his opponent made the shot. *He definitely will not try and follow the ball.* He will not and cannot keep his eye on the ball until he has made contact and returned the volley. If he does attempt to chase the ball with his eyes, he will be late for every fast shot.

So how does a player hit the fast ball? Essentially he must anticipate the motions of his opponent. The sooner the shot is called and correctly judged, the sooner the player can get his body to the vicinity of the ball where he can make a shot. There are degrees of anticipation. Some players are so skillful that they can judge a shot by their opponent's stroke. Most do not employ such tactics. The purpose of early anticipation is to be prepared for the shot so the player doesn't have to see the ball as it approaches the hitting zone. Analyze the service — will it be a flat serve, a slice, or a twist? The adjustment must be made before the ball actually traverses the net.

Once the player reaches the ball, he must hit the ball in front of his body and always try to be aggressive. We say try, because in reality you never know where you are hitting the ball in relation to the arc of your swing. However, you must remember that the faster the ball, the farther forward you must move because you only know the trajectory of the ball and never its precise location to the racquet.

So a beginner of intermediate tennis must learn how to cope with speed and not apply slow-game fundamentals to the fast game. Most tennis teaching is done in slow motion and does not apply to the fast game.

Fast tennis requires:
   early anticipation
2) abandoning the trajectory of the oncoming ball so the eyes are not forced to follow the ball
3) shortening the swing to make a faster shot
4) striking the ball as early as possible.

The major fault of players trying to adjust to speed is that shots are hit late. The tennis player fails to anticipate and is not fully set for the shot. At times a full swing is attempted when there is no time for it.

There is an amount of guesswork to the fast game. The trajectory is seen and then lost. The longer one delays the shot, by trying to follow the ball, the greater will be the margin of error. In slow tennis, there is time for deliberation but not in fast tennis. It is a different game, with different strokes, and different visual demands. It is the more challenging and exciting game and belongs to the better player.

● Hitting on the move impairs your vision

Running is one of the great spoilers of vision. It is simple to demonstrate this point. If you hold a newspaper in your hand and try to run on the spot, your ability to read the print will be impaired. The faster you run, the more impaired your vision. It is not possible to jog and read at the same time.

In tennis, the visual demands are not as critical, as a ball is fairly large. You don't need great vision to see a tennis ball — after all, you are not attempting to read the label on the ball. You need good vision because there are so many spoilers to good sight despite a healthy-sized target. These visual spoilers are running, acceleration, eye movement and, of course, the speed of the ball.

With a fast-moving ball, this loss of visual acuity during running may mean that the ball is lost early, soon after your opponent makes contact. The ball is in flight and is seen only as a blur. As it approaches, even the trajectory or flight pattern of the ball may be lost. If the player were standing still, he might see the ball more clearly. But distinct vision is hampered by running.

Tennis is a moving game. It seems, to the casual observer, that the tennis player is constantly moving in a fluid motion sweeping from one side of the court to the other. The professional may seem to do this but, in fact, the better player attempts to achieve visual stability by arriving at the point he will make contact early, stopping, and thus removing one of the major variables of blurred vision — the moving body.

There are several styles of running. Some people seem to glide and take long smooth strokes and although they move quickly, they do so smoothly and with minimal visual loss. Some players run like a piston, churning up and down and the body displacement is maximal — their visual interference is also high. There are even tennis players who run blindly, with their face to the ground as though they were doing an intense dash. They have little opportunity to see their opponent hit and cannot then adjust properly. And there are variations to these patterns. Some tennis players seem to be lazy, start out slow, realize they are not going to make it to the ball, and put forth a great deal of speed. The burst of speed coincides with the time the ball is hit so the visual turmoil is high. Then there is the player who is so hyperexcitable that he charges every ball like a bull going for the cape. He rarely sees the ball and invariably finds himself cramped for a shot because he has run into the hitting zone of the ball. Such a player rushes around the court, attacks each ball, and never can properly execute any shot. On the other side of this personality type is the phlegmatic soul who sees the ball well as he takes a few cosy strides to it — but frequently doesn't reach it. He sees the ball quite well because his acceleration is slow and he runs with a glide — but his pace is too slow for the game.

Ideally a player should glide with long, smooth running strokes with the eyes directed toward the opponent's court. The fast part of the "run" should be early. In the perfect play, the player is there to receive the ball with both feet on the ground so that there is little head and body displacement. Most players do well to stop the forward acceleration of their body with one foot on the ground. They avoid the loss of vision which results at high speeds.

Why is the visual loss not self-correcting? Certainly if one needed glasses to drive, then the loss of those glasses would necessitate getting a new pair. There is an immediate recognition of the loss of visual acuity. In tennis, or with running, it doesn't happen. A player in motion isn't aware that his movements are reducing his acuity down to partially sighted levels. It is appalling how low the vision can drop with fast running — certainly to the level of legal blindness. This does not mean loss of light perception but rather the inability to see images at twenty feet that a normal person can see at 200 feet. The tennis player is so accustomed to seeing poorly when he plays that he accepts it as the norm. He can also complete his tasks. He can still find the ball in the court, hit the ball without a miss, and do his tennis work despite these visual slips. But, he may be late for shots or misdirect them because his visual judgement is off.

Good players do not make special visual efforts to play the game. Through trial and error they learn how to run, they discover the proper speed and acceleration and the timing to carry them to the ball so at least one foot is stable and the head no longer has any up-and-down motion. The cessation of motion of body and head stabilizes their vision. What they are doing is improving their visual performance which in a fast game is critical — frequently the difference between hitting accurately or poorly. On a return of service, the player that can see the ball a little longer than his opponent is often the player who can break a service.

How can a player become more conscious of the role of his eyes? If a player plays against a ball machine, his body is relatively stable and the visual demands small. The same effect is produced during warm-ups. There are some players who are fantastic during warm-up exercises prior to a tennis match and then go on to get soundly thrashed as soon as their opponent realizes they are poor players if they are forced to move. These players do well against ball machines or against middle-of-the-court warm-up exercises and do poorly on the move because they have running-visual problems. They are moving either too fast, too awkwardly, too erratically. At any rate, they are ruining their visual control of the game which precludes hitting a fast ball properly or getting the body to a proper distance from the ball to allow a swing that is neither stretched nor cramped.

The best way to see yourself move and correct your running game is through video tapes. By improving your running game, you can improve your sharpness of vision although all the visual blurring which is a natural conse-quence of a fast game cannot be eliminated.

2 How The Eye Sees

All sports, to varying degrees, require sharp vision of the players. Having normal vision may not guarantee that the eyes will be comfortable and effective throughout a full game. Hyperopia and astigmatism can cause eyestrain in long matches resulting in ocular muscle spasm, blinking, tearing, photophobia, and even double vision. In a long match the cumulative effect of eyestrain will cause a player to tire as the competition progresses so that he is not at his best and becomes fatigued. When games are played at night or under inadequate light, visual problems may become exaggerated.

Coaches today are quite sophisticated and use the latest equipment, techniques in coaching, and training methods. However, they are often unaware of the physiology of vision, the nature of defective vision, and what can be done to correct deficient eyesight. They are often unaware of how one's visual concentration can be improved and how to utilize natural physiological behaviors of central and peripheral vision, eye dominance, and depth perception to the advantage of the player.

 Central vision

We have two basic types of vision: central and peripheral vision. The receptors of our fine central vision lie in an area of the retina called the macula: the macula is proportionate in size to the retina as the area of Toronto is to Canada. Here six million ganglion cells or cones relay the central portion of our vision to the brain so that a picture of the world is formed. These cones are able to interpret colour and determine contrast of colour.

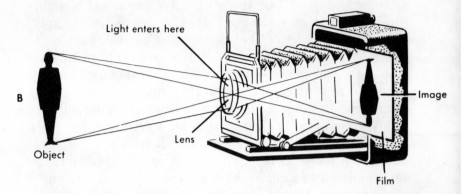

Light enters here

B

Image

Object

Lens

Film

The eye is like a camera in which the target object is focused upside down on the sensory cells or retina of the eye. Like an automatic camera with automatic focusing, the eye can adjust its focus and automatically control the light input.

Around the perimeter of the retina are rods which are responsible for our peripheral vision. These are not as finely tuned and do not perceive the same high level of quality and colour that is perceived in the central macular area. It is the central vision that one refers to as 20/20.

The Snellen chart is commonly used to determine visual acuity. Letters are graded so that they subtend a small angle of five minutes of arc which gives the familiar 20/20 that we refer to as normal vision. Notations are made so that inferior vision, such as 20/40 vision, would indicate that a person could see at twenty feet what a person with normal eyesight could identify at forty feet. While 20/20 is considered normal there are individuals who will see 20/15 readily (superior vision) and others who will not see beyond 20/30. These levels of vision are considered to be within the normal range of the population. Certainly someone who has 20/15 vision, which means he can see at twenty feet what a normal person could perceive at fifteen feet, will have much superior acuity on the courts. We discovered Eddie Dibbs could see 20/15 readily with his soft contact lenses. This superior vision means better effectiveness on the courts; Connors is said to have this type of extraordinary central visual acuity.

While a loss of acuity in central vision cannot be recovered, it can be improved if there are errors of refraction or errors within the system of the eye that can be corrected by a spectacle or contact lens. Very often there are small errors of astigmatism hyperopia, or myopia that go unnoticed in one or both eyes. Fine correction by an eye physician can improve the visual acuity in topnotch athletes from 20/30 to 20/15. In an interesting study at Texas A & M University, the shooting ability of basketball players was directly related to the visual acuity of the athlete. One of the conclusions reached was that a topnotch player could be identified early in his career by determining his degree of shooting accuracy predicated on his visual acuity.

Thus we see that the better an athlete's vision, the better chance he has to excel in sports. This is particularly true in tennis where the visual aspects of the game are of fundamental importance. The player must be able to follow his opponent's stroke and accurately gauge the trajectory of the ball.

Central static acuity is the aspect of vision that discriminates colour. Colour is very important in tennis. Only a few years ago the white ball was the only colour permitted on the courts but today yellow, pink, and orange balls are popular. Players with poor colour discrimination would find the game becoming progressively difficult as the white ball picked up the colour of the court surface, or lose the ball against the white shirt of their opponents.

Even today the yellow ball, without fine discrimination of our central vision, may be lost against the clouds and sky, particularly on a day bright with sunshine. Our central acuity can be sharpened by wearing sunglasses that have a yellow haze filter; contrast will be heightened and the yellow ball will appear white in colour.

Ted Williams, the outstanding baseball batter, was reportedly able to see the seams of a baseball from the instant it left the pitcher's hand at eighty mph. This is the stuff of living legends but has little regard for visual physiology.

● Dynamic visual acuity

We have discussed our ability to see from a stationary position. We can see clearly while at rest but, if we are moving as is so often the case in tennis, our visual acuity drops off considerably. Some simple tests will demonstrate how your vision falls off while you are in motion: 1) Place a record on the turntable. At thirty-three rpm you should be able to read the label of the album. When the speed is changed to forty-five rpm only the large print can be distinguished. At seventy-eight rpm, all print is a blur. 2) Look at a poster on the far side of a room then run on the spot and see how much of the poster you can read. You will be surprised at the reduction in vision. 3) When you next see a movie, try to read the list of credits. If the print is too small and the credits roll by too fast, you will not be able to decipher them.

How, then, can a player identify the ball while he is running? He cannot. He must run to the point where he anticipates the ball will be played so he has time to await the ball. He will no longer depend on dynamic visual acuity but, when stationary, will use his static visual acuity. That is why coaches will so often say, "Be there ahead of time, anticipate, be ready." By anticipating and awaiting the ball, you can improve your visual perception remarkably and consequently improve your game.

 Visual memory

We know the world through only our memory and recall. If we had not seen a ball before, we could not label one as such. Similarly, if we have not experienced different spins on a ball, the direction a ball with a particular kind of spin might take after the bounce, we would have no idea of how to anticipate from what we see. So when we play, we look for ideas stored in our memory of images. Our memory helps analyse an opponent's shot and dictates how we must move and when in order to make the proper return.

When we see the ball as it leaves the racquet of our opponent, we must make split-second observations and draw upon our recall to correctly determine the speed, depth, and spin of the ball. We must focus our total attention on the ball while it is in our opponent's court.

Visual memory also plays a role in recall of where the opponent's court lines are. When we hit the ball, we know not only by the feel of the hit but also by our recall of the opponent's court lines as to whether the ball will be in bounds or out. We must often make shots blindly; that is, we cannot be looking directly at the net but our visual recall helps us to adjust our shot to the height of the net. This recall is as important in tennis as is memory recall in other sports. In basketball, players will often shoot at the basket without even so much as seeing the basket but are able to shoot by reflex by having visual recall of the basket. Similarly, in golf, holes-in-one are often made when the hole is not in sight but by visual recall of where the hole is. Experiments have shown that by visualizing in any particular sport the muscles that may be involved with that particular activity will actually conform to a certain pattern depending on the visual memory. This has been referred to as "muscle memory."

You can use visual memory to your advantage in tennis. For example, before you serve, visually recall the complete serve and go through all the motions mentally. Seeing the ball leave the hand, going up in the air, reaching its peak, being hit, going over the net, and falling on the opponent's side will be a great help when you go to serve. Players who have used this method find that when they go to play it becomes like playing in slow motion. It will appear to them that they have more time to hit the ball correctly and properly follow through. Thus, where possible, make a mental recall of the complete mechanics of the stroke.

Concentration also plays an important part in visual memory and visual recall. For example, if we were driving down a street looking for a street sign but were distracted, even though we might see it we might pass it by. We must learn to concentrate on what we are trying to remember so that the combination of concentration and visual recall will reinforce the visual imagery and object of regard. In that manner, we are able to strengthen our vision and play better.

 Visual constancy

Our visual memory takes us one step further so that we are in a position to identify objects as constants. Owing to the structure of the eye, to its continuous motion even during strong attempts at fixation, and its continuing change in state of accommodation, the retinal image or the image cast on the back of the eye is tiny, upside-down, variably blurred, wiggling, and jerking. In fact, there really never is a strong image on the retina at all but a continuous pattern of ever-changing images. Yet our experience of vision is static and we regard objects and structures in the world as constants.

Objects in space keep their size, shape, colour, and speed despite large variations in the retinal image to which they correspond. Turn your head sharply. The stimulus on the back of the eye is such that there should be a blurred movement in the visual fields rather like the picture from a camera moved as the shutter is opened. However, as we perceive, the surroundings remain relatively still.

This size constancy can be demonstrated by standing in front of a slightly steamed mirror and tracing the image of one's head on the surface. By moving back and looking at the outline, it will appear much smaller than it truly is. It is precisely half the size of our head. Yet we do not see a difference because our visual memory recalls the size of our head. Without constancy of size we would see man double in height after a few steps toward us and, when he extended his hand in a greeting, it would appear enormous in our field of vision just as it does to a movie camera. But our brain unconsciously reduces the size of all objects to what it remembers. This has bearing not only in watching the ball and observing it through its various stages where it always remains the identical size, but also in our fundamental grasp of the opponent's court area which does not shift in size no matter where our position in the field be it at the net or at the baseline.

The same constancy applies to shape. We can demonstrate this by holding a book so that the flat surface is horizontal and somewhat below eye level. The shape of the surface now looks rectangular but if an attempt is made to draw it, the shape will be seen not as rectangular but as a trapezoid. Our retina and brain perceive this so that it remains constant for us.

Speed also remains a constant. The brain adjusts for the ball's acceleration so that we notice a change in speed hardly at all. This is unlike a camera to which the speed change would be very noticeable throughout the flight of the ball.

 ## Ocular dominance

Each of us has one eye which is our master eye and dominates our aim. If this eye were impaired or obstructed we would be off considerably in our orientation to space. Try keeping both eyes open and looking at a distant object such as a telephone pole, chimney, or some such target. Then alternately close each eye. You will notice that one eye will be directly on target with the viewing object while the other eye is off several inches, and you will have to reposition yourself to line up with the target. The eye that is lined up when both eyes are open is considered to be the dominant eye.

A great deal has been written concerning the laterality of the dominant eye. There is no direct correlation that a right-handed person has his right eye dominant or a left-handed person has a left eye dominant, nor is there any correlation that an opposite hand-eye correlation has any advantage over a hand-eye dominance of the same side. While it is easy to determine which eye is the dominant eye, there may at times be some difficulty in determining the hand with which the player is dominant. For instance, Eddie Dibbs plays right-handed tennis but performs all other motor skills such as eating and writing with his left hand. In this sense, he is ambidextrous but yet he has a right-hand dominance for the sport of tennis.

Robert Bedard was ranked number one for many years in Canada and on the international circuit. He claims that his errors increase when hitting the tennis ball on the side of the non-dominant eye. Is the alignment of the dominant eye obstructed in these instances so that the non-dominant eye must come into play to a greater extent on the non-dominant side? It is possible that in some of the volley shots and over-head smashes the arm and racquet may be in the way of the dominant eye so that the small impairment in visual orienta-tion that occurs from the non-dominant eye may come into play which will increase the margin of error. This single fact of hitting at times using only the poor sighting device of the non-dominant eye may account for a number of lost points in a tennis match.

 ## Peripheral vision

Peripheral vision is most important in the game of tennis. As mentioned previously, our eyes have central vision consisting of cones. Our peripheral vision is made up of small, tiny rods. By far the larger area is our peripheral vision. Hold your hands out to the sides of your body and move your fingers with your eyes looking straight ahead. You can see on both sides to the horizontal 180 degrees and watch your fingers move. Except for a small area called the blind spot, which corresponds to the entrance of the optic nerve into our eye, we have full peripheral vision extending out to 180 degrees. It is this peripheral vision that permits us to run for the ball and yet, at the same time, know where our partner in a doubles match is located. Were it not for this peripheral vision, we would be frequently bumping into our partner. It is through this peripheral vision we first glimpse our partner's shot as it is unleashed behind us.

The rods in our peripheral vision have the ability to detect only black and white vision. They have no colour discrimination. Yet, when we lie on our back and look up to the sky, we see the whole sky as blue including that in the periphery of our vision. How is this possible? This is possible through our memory recall combined with the coordination of our central visual acuity which can determine colour. Thus a combination of central and peripheral vision which is present for everyone gives us our fine discrimination in size, shape, and colour.

A number of studies have been done to show the change in our peripheral field when one is in motion. Many of these studies have been done with the motorist in mind. A person going fifty-five miles per hour has his visual field reduced by two-thirds so that he has only a sixty degree field of vision as compared to a full 180 degree field. Thus in tennis, when you are moving fast, your visual field contracts considerably which is to your disadvantage. If you are able to anticipate where the ball will be hit and arrive in the ready and stationary position, you have a much wider visual field and can readily identify your opponent's position. This enables you to make a passing shot or a strategic shot to your advantage. If you are still running to the ball, your peripheral field becomes so contracted that you are not able to see where your opponent is moving to.

 Eyestrain

Eyestrain is a condition that develops when a person is constantly striving to see. When a game is continued for a number of sets, eyestrain may set in which will lead to poor judgement, poor depth perception, a lack of fusion and general and ocular fatigue. In addition, eyestrain may result from poor oxygenation of the brain and the neuromuscular component of the eyes which could lead to late visual responses. The eye muscles start to pull and feel knotted up. The constant change of focus from far to near and vice versa may periodically give temporary blurring of vision and a sense of visual confusion. Fatigue can seriously impair performance by impairing visual acuity and visual responsiveness. There may also be restrictions and contractions in the visual field which would be very significant in doubles play.

What causes eyestrain in tennis players? Certainly, any game that is taxing, and extends over any length of time, can produce a certain amount of ocular fatigue. The ocular muscles with their "to and fro motion," and the fine muscles that control the accommodative reflex which have to focus for near and far, will eventually fatigue. This leads to "staring" and lack of blinking which in turn produces a form of drying and dehydration of the cornea or outer layer of the eye. This in turn will produce a fogging effect on vision and lack of definition of objects will result.

One factor that will contribute to eyestrain is any uncorrected refractive error that should be corrected by spectacles or contact lenses. Also, some players will have a poor fusional mechanism, that is, a mechanism by which they are able to see the ball with both eyes working in unison. This fusional mechanism requires an unconscious effort to maintain binocular vision and depth perception and if this fusional effort is great, the eyes will fatigue readily during a long set.

Illumination is also important. If the illumination is inadequate for the visual task, the definition of the ball will be affected and this will produce eyestrain. On some days when the sky is bright, if there is a large number of overhead shots, an extremely strong fusional effort on the part of the eye will become very difficult to prolong and the eyes will tire readily. In some cases, there is a small muscle imbalance between one eye and the other, and when fatigue sets in fusion breaks down and blurring of vision occurs. The lids may tire in response to constant squinting to control the glare of the sun.

The upward gaze, necessary for the large number of serves during a match in close sets or a large number of overheads, may produce eyestrain and fatigue. Try looking up ten times in a row and notice how tired the eyes feel. Gazing upwards stretches our eye muscles to the limit and this is a position the eyes are not readily accustomed to.

To avoid excessive eyestrain, general fitness must be advocated because exercise has well known beneficial effects on heart, lung, and muscular conditioning. Swimming, walking, jogging, and bicycle riding are all useful vehicles for attaining better conditioning. However, tennis players must play tennis. The visual side of the game is a mix of anticipation and vision. Without practice, the perfect mix will never occur. Besides illumination, the practice of trying to follow fast-moving objects is the other major way of improving dynamic visual acuity. A great tennis player should be a good runner.

A momentary rest between matches is also helpful. Rest is the obvious antidote to fatigue. But a player does not have the luxury of a long pause between matches. However, the game can be slowed down just simply by taking longer to retrieve balls and by doing some blinking exercises between matches. With any concentrated activity, the blink rate goes drastically down be it reading or driving a car. In fact, the blink rate may drop from sixteen to twenty times per minute to four or five times. Fatigue often ensues when the eyes do not blink because of drying of the front surface of the eye, the cornea, and lack of polishing which normally clears away debris to make optical surface of the eye more regular. Ten quick blinks may polish, hydrate, and generally refresh the eyes and is useful exercise for tired tennis players, weary drivers and glassy-eyed students. The same effect could be achieved with ordinary eyedrops, collyria, but why bother with the cost and inconvenience of eyedrops when the most natural and best lubricant is your tears.

Hearing the ball

As there are profound limitations to following a tennis ball, every bit of sensory input is important to the brain's ability to accurately compute the correct trajectory of the ball. Sensory information is mixed, so hearing, for example, can improve your vision. Musicians speak of "blue" notes, as if the sounds possessed colour. Decorators refer to the "warm, earthy" colours of beige or orange as if they had a tactile quality. For a tennis player, the sound of the ball helps him to locate it in space. Try playing tennis when an airplane flies overhead or a train whistles by. Not only will the sound be distracting, but it will eliminate one of the most important localizing clues to the ball's flight. It is therefore easier to compute the course of the ball after it has bounced. You can never be sure of this moment from visual information. That is why there are so many line disputes in a tennis game. Players arguing over what each is sure he saw, will go to the disputed spot looking for a ball mark to back up his claim. It is one of the thorns of tennis, since most players readily believe what they think they see.

Again, you can be confident of the time and place of the bounce if the ball is travelling slowly. As we have said, high-speed balls cannot be seen in certain positions, but they can always be heard. The thud of the tennis ball is a characteristic sound which helps to tell you where it is. On fast, hard asphalt courts the sound is loud, whereas on slower clay, it is muffled.

For the professionals who have to play the fast game, audience and background noise are serious obstacles to play. This is why so many professionals become angry when they have to return a serve when there is heckling and jeering going on behind them. Someone who has to face Roscoe Tanner, who has one of the fastest serves in modern tennis, needs the auditory information to complement the meagre visual slips of information that the blistering ball is going to give. Without a sound, the correct localization of the ball in space is more difficult. At least, the sensory information of hearing is strong and reliable whereas the visual information is illusory and tends to breed overconfidence because of each player's trust in his eyes.

One useful exercise in the development of dynamic visual acuity is to play with ear plugs. It makes the game more difficult but certainly sharpens one's eye to follow a fast-moving ball without the aid of auditory clues.

3 The Game

● Impact — the ball striking the racquet is a
non-visual event

Only high-speed photography can freeze the instant of
impact of a tennis ball on the racquet. Many current coaching
techniques are predicated on the feasability that the eyes are
so acute they can follow the flight of the ball to impact but this
is impossible in the fast game. A player should concentrate on
the orientation of his racquet — is it perpendicular or slanted?

*Eddie Dibbs attempts a high two-handed volley. The ball has passed out of his
field of direct vision and impact is a blind event.*

A player should know where on the rise of the ball he will make contact, where in the arc of his swing he will make the hit. He should know how long a ball will stay on the strings, especially for spinners. Unfortunately, the eyes cannot provide the necessary data to allow the player to make the successful stroke. These are meaningless coaching techniques because the eye cannot see the impact of the ball and the racquet.

It is possible, through experience, to develop skills to make the proper shot. The point is a player cannot rely upon sight to prove the most dramatic moment in tennis — that moment when the ball hits the racquet. The actual stroke occurs far too fast for the eye to see.

Some players claim they can see the ball right into the racquet. If you are one of these players, search your visual memory for an image of what the ball looks like when it smashes into the gut. Is there a slight separation of the gut at impact? Does the gut bend? Does the racquet face vibrate?

Some players claim they can watch the ball almost to the point of impact. How far away? An inch, perhaps six inches, maybe a foot? Consider the serve: When do you no longer see the ball coming at you — a distance of three feet, maybe six or ten? Nobody knows. No one is really sure.

Why do the claims of players about their visual control of the ball vary so greatly? The answer has two components: When the ball can be seen is a factor of speed and also of the acuteness of dynamic vision. Dynamic vision depends upon contrast, good illumination, ability to concentrate, and static acuity — the ability to see clearly with the eye at rest. If a player is tired, worried, preoccupied, playing at twilight, or not wearing distance glasses, he will not see the ball early.

Some players state that they can see the seams of the ball, or its label, or the fuzzy texture of the ball as it sails through the air at eighty miles an hour. But if you can see details on the ball in its maximum flight, you should be able to read the newspaper while you are jogging. Most people can't do it just running on the spot.

So impact is non-visual event. Who cares?

Well, it should lift a burden off many tennis students.

There are those tennis teachers who give specific instructions about hitting the ball at impact. Yes, you should hit the ball in the middle of the racquet but in reality you reach out with your racquet and take what you can get. If the ball pops up, you have hit the ball on the edge of the racquet; if the racquet twists in your hand and feels like a tuning fork, then the ball is near the edge of the racquet; if the sound is a nice thud with good gut resonance and the ball goes where you want it to, it is probably at or near the center of the racquet. But why worry if your racquet is vertical at impact or slightly tilted? You can't see the impact so forget it. It is another weight off your tennis back. Are you uptight about hitting the ball on the rise or at its summit? Relax, your concern is over. You can't really tell. On a half volley, where does your racquet scoop up the ball? Who knows? It's a blind act. If you are photographed taking a half volley, you will discover your eyes gaze to the front and are not even looking at the ball at the site of the bounce prior to impact.

To properly play this fast game of tennis, it is vital that you stop pretending that your eyes can witness all the action in the game.

Is there anything a player can do who has only fair dynamic visual acuity? This would include those players in good health, who do not take medications, sleep seven to eight hours at night, and play tennis only once or twice a week.

The big racquet has to be seriously considered. And it has been seriously considered. Dr. Howard Brody, a physicist at the University of Pennsylvania, reported his findings in the *American Journal of Physics* about the physics of a tennis racquet. His tennis talk was not typical locker-room discussion as it revolved around percussion centers, vibration nodes, dwell times, asymmetric deflections, and restitution coefficients. He brought to bear the full thrust of a physics laboratory to do his tests on the racquet and impact employing laser beams, mirrors, and oscilliscopes.

His results were remarkably similar to Howard Head's, the remarkable man who not only invented the Head Ski, but the large sized Prince racquet. Dr. Brody found that the center of percussion, a vital factor in racquet performance, varied from racquet to racquet. The percussion center is that spot on the racquet which, if hit by a ball, will not produce vibration or torque — areas called vibration nodes. If torque occurs, the racquet twists in the hand which strains the muscles of the forearm and is one of the principal causes of tennis elbow. Torque also reduces the accuracy of return. The percussion center should be in the center of the racquet head, but Dr. Brody found it was an eccentric area, somewhat displaced by an inch or so closer to the handle. In larger racquets, the

John McEnroe makes contact with the sweet spot of the racquet. Note his head is not even turned to the ball.

percussion center is larger and tends to be more centrally placed with an extension toward the shaft of the racquet.

The percussion center is often called the "sweet spot" because it is the best place to hit a ball on the racquet head. The sweet spot is the center of percussion, the point on the face where impact produced no vibration at the end of the handle.

If the ball strikes the racquet on a line perpendicular to it, the ball will rebound straight or at an 180-degree line. But if the ball hits the racquet at an off-center point, the ball will rebound at an angle. The farther from the sweet spot the ball makes contact with the racquet, the farther askew it will go. So the direction of the ball coming off the racquet can be changed radically according to the place on the racquet head the ball is hit. Of course, the path of the returned ball does not simply depend on the exact position of impact on the racquet but on the inclination of the racquet. If at impact the racquet is tilted back, the ball will rise and tend to go long — if it is tilted down, the ball will head into the net. Ideally then, to have the best combination, the ball should strike the sweet spot at the moment the racquet is vertical. As we have said, it is not possible to see this happen, but the player can insure that his grip is strong so that tilting does not occur because of the force of the ball.

Dr. Brody also found that the energy of the oncoming ball is not radically dissipated by its collision with the gut or nylon of the racquet. The distance of the ball's rebound is determined by its coefficient of restitution. This is the ratio of velocity after collision to the velocity before the collision. He found that the kinetic energy of the tennis ball is only lost by a half with impact. Howard Head also studied the coefficient of restitution and discovered that the return velocity of a ball struck at an area outside the sweet spot zone could be one-third to one-half of the velocity of a ball being returned from the central area. Moreover on his own Prince racquet he found a very high velocity return area close to the throat of the racquet that was not present on other tennis racquets. This meant that not only was direction of the ball more true after hitting the sweet spot, but the force of return power was greater after impact in this area.

In effect, the center of percussion and the center of the racquet should coincide so that the longest carrying hit is also the one that produces the least vibration.

Dr. Brody, using a laser beam, measured the duration of impact and found it was only five milliseconds. This incredibly short interval does not permit the eye to see what is happening. The time cycle is slightly greater when one considers the time taken for the racquet head to bend back when hit by the ball and return to its normal position. The dwell time — the time that the ball stays in contact with the gut — is shortened, however, if the racquet is strung tighter.

Most of the events at impact require laser beams or strobe photography to detail the happening. As impact is not seen, it makes sense to have a racquet that is larger, with a larger sweet spot and greater area for optimum hitting when the ball can be returned without losing its power or direction. Great players do not need the benefit from the larger surface as much as average or club players. The professionals or top amateurs have the anticipation, the fast moves, the sharpness of excellent dynamic acuity, and the proper strokes to insure that the ball will be returned effectively. The intermediates, while playing the fast game, are frequently unable to cope with the accelerated demands of a brief hitting time. They hit while on the run, do not read the signals of their opponent's next shot correctly, and they move without proper timing so that they are reaching for the ball totally outstretched, or run right into the ball and have to hug their elbow into their body to complete a swing. They make errors because they don't have the conditioning or coordination to deal with a hot tennis ball. When they finally are required to make their shot, they are not ready for it and the ball can strike the racquet at any place. The larger racquet area does not correct the essential faults in the game but it does assist the player to increase the odds that the most optimum area of the racquet surface will be hit.

● Is the large racquet an antidote to blind impact?

The big racquet has been accused by its critics of making the game too easy. It is true that the design of the head takes some of the insecurity out of hitting, but the game really doesn't become simpler. It has allowed more people to enjoy and play the fast game and keep the ball in motion for extended play. An average player merely increases his probability of returning the ball for a return of service on a during net play. He can do things with a big racquet that would be difficult or impossible with a smaller racquet head. The difference in size between a large racquet such as the Prince and a conventional racquet is only two inches in width. The length is the same as both are twenty-seven inches. However, the effective size of the sweet spot on this larger racquet head is almost twice the size when compared to an ordinary racquet. The big racquets look longer but it is an optical illusion because the width has been increased while the height has remained constant. They are not especially elegant and they look somewhat like a primitive club.

One advantage of this racquet occurs in serving. On groundstrokes the wrist is held firm and the racquet's speed relatively constant throughout the arc of the swing. Extra power on a service is gained by a wrist snap which speeds up the velocity of the head of the racquet. With oversized racquets the extra dimension of the sweet spot is at the throat of the racquet. So not only is the groundstroke aided, but also the overhead smash of a serve.

The large racquet has the same wind resistance as the smaller ones. It is not heavier nor is it awkward because of balance. The swing is somewhat altered as there is not the same degree of manouverability. Players who first employ it require some adaptation or breaking-in to compensate for the slightly different swing. Those players who regularly employ a lot of wrist in their shots find the oversized racquet less responsive. However, on balance, the advantages of larger surface to insure stability and proper impact outweigh the disadvantages of greater bulk. Some of the top professionals such as Pam Shriver have used it, but the large racquet has really come into its own as a choice of the average club player. There is a certain sheepishness about using the big racquet as it still bears some of the ridicule of being a cheater racquet elevating the calibre of a player's game without any discernable change occurring in strokes or tactics. However, this resistance is being overcome as more and more large racquets are being used.

In doubles play, where the net play is crucial to the success of the game, the big racquet offers considerable advantages. It is better protection for the face. In tennis, most injuries occur at the net because the velocity of the ball is so great. The larger the racquet surface, the better the coverage for the face and especially the eyes. Even the stroke for net play is frequently a frontal blocking motion where the velocity of the return depends entirely upon the speed of the oncoming ball, the tilt of the racquet, and the position of impact. So a fast ball coming off the sweet spot can have double the speed of a ball coming off near the margin of the frame. In a blocking motion, the player imparts very little of his own power to the return, so the site of impact is the major factor which determines whether a ball dribbles off or deflects sharply from a block hit.

There is no doubt that the large-framed racquets are here to stay. They improve the ability of a player to cope with the vagaries of blind impact. They are especially useful for club players with inherent weaknesses in their game and should be the racquet of choice for doubles players. They add stability to wrist and forearm and decrease the likelihood of torque which is prone to occur when a fast ball hits the margin of the racquet surface. Any player who has tennis elbow or is prone to tennis elbow must be appreciative of this particular advantage. It can be enjoyed by men and women alike because the added size is not accompanied by added weight. They feel light although they suffer the initial impression of looking heavy and cumbersome. The transfer of play from a small racquet to a larger one is not always an inspiring occasion. The added size definitely requires a breaking-in period as the rhythm of the swing is changed especially for those players who use the wrist in providing topspin. Many players also find it awkward if their game is based on the serve, as initially a bulkier racquet does not seem to whip as easily as a smaller one.

The big racquet provides realistic solutions imposed by the

problem of the visual limitations of impact. Naturally, they do not help a player see better, but they do increase the probability that this blind climax will be more successfully dispatched. For a while, it seemed that small racquet faces were the trend. But the big ones are definitely now in vogue. They make sense — the wonder of it is that they took so long in coming.

The big racquet is popular with tennis players because its added dimensions and the enlarged sweet spot reduce errors of timing and those caused by poor fitness. It has enjoyed the endorsement of the touring professionals: it can deliver a blazing serve and is quite effective for slicing or spinning the ball. Some players find the large racquet cumbersome because they must use excessive topspin to avoid over-hitting and sending the ball out of bounds. The large racquet solves many problems, including a fundamental loss of visual control which occurs when hitting the ball takes place. It is not for everyone and indeed when playing tennis becomes automatic and anticipation becomes more important than seeing, the strengths of such a racquet becomes less important. Chuck Kriese, the coach of the Junior Davis Cup team, finds the Prince racquet strong on serve and claims that five out of ten 1980 team members used this racquet. Gene Mayer uses the Prince Graphite and credits his tennis success and its use (*Tennis Magazine,* June 1980). The big racquet and its enlarged sweet spot is probably the best remedy for blind impact.

● Visual clues at the baseline, net, on return of serve

The great tennis players move for the ball even before their opponent makes his shot. In the fast game, if a player waits until the ball is travelling back to him, chances are he will be unable to play the ball. The ball is much easier to see in the distance and the longer a player waits to make his move, the harder it will be for him to clearly follow the path of the ball. Anticipation begins by observing the motions of your opponent. Because your opponent may be as far away as 100 feet, you need good vision to see your adversary clearly.

The slower the game the more time one has to rely upon visual clues in order to prepare for the next shot. If a ball is hit easily, the eye will be able to follow the ball after its bounce regardless of spin on it. Also, you will not need to move at top speed so your eyesight will be more accurate.

However, if you enjoy the challenge of the fast game, you need to respond to the ball quickly. At fast speeds, the eyes are not competent to fixate on the ball. What you lose visually you must make up for by gauging the direction, velocity, and bounce of the ball before it hits the surface.

The importance of anticipation can be illustrated very simply when playing against a ball machine. After each shot, you are well aware of the general area the ball will hit, regardless of speed. These predictable shots, although fast, are easier to cope with than the mix of shots your opponent can deliver.

Visual clues give information as to the nature of the oncoming ball, that is, whether the ball will be short or deep, high or low, fast or slow. A player can also determine the direction the ball is travelling and, by watching his opponent's stroke, what type of spin is on the ball. The quicker a player can analyze the visual clues, the greater are his chances of making a successful return.

Visual clues are received by a player in the "ready" position. There are three different locations for the "ready" position:
1) at the baseline in anticipation of hitting a forehand or backhand groundstroke;
2) at the net in anticipation of hitting a volley or overhead;
3) in position to return service.

 ## Visual clues at the baseline

How deep in your own court you can expect to play the ball can be determined by the nature of your opponent's follow-through and the height that the ball travels over the net. If your opponent completely follows through, and the ball travels at least three feet over the net, the ball will land deep in your court. If your opponent has a short follow-through, and/or the ball barely skims over the net, it will land shallow in the court.

The spin on the oncoming ball can be determined by the

nature of your opponent's swing. A player whose racquet travels up the back of the ball will be hitting with overspin or topspin. A player whose racquet travels down the back of the ball will be hitting with underspin. If the swing carries straight through the ball, the player will be hitting flat. Being able to recognize the type of spin on the ball is an important visual clue that will help you to respond properly to the shot.

 ## Topspin

The topspin ball has a higher bounce than the other spin balls. Hard-hit topspin balls tend to stay in the court due to the nature of the spin. The topspin can be recognized by a racquet swing which travels from a low to high position, and by the motion of the wrist which whips the racquet face up the back of the ball. Topspin can be put on forehand or backhand shots although most average players find that the forehand topspin is the easier shot to hit.

 ## Underspin

The underspin ball has a lower bounce and a slower speed after the bounce than other spin balls. The racquet swing begins high and comes down across the back of the ball. It is commonly employed as a routine backhand shot, since it is easier to hit than the topspin shot, and for tactical shots such as the defensive lob, the approach shot, and the drop shot.

 ## Flat ball

After it bounces, the speed of the flat ball will be almost the same as its speed prior to striking the surface. The flat ball must narrowly clear the net for it to land safely in the court. It is for this reason that the shot tends to be more difficult to consistently hit than, for example, the topspin shot.

By closely scrutinizing the racquet swing of your opponent, you can visually anticipate how the ball will respond as it bounces and hence get into the best possible position for a successful return.

 ## Visual clues at the net

Being able to determine the type of spin on the ball is of great importance when at the net. Take, for example, a situation where a player is in position at the net and his opponent has attempted a passing shot that has been hit relatively hard and at least five feet above the net. Will the ball land safely or out of the court? The answer depends on the type of spin on the ball. If the ball is hit with topspin there is a good chance it will land in and hence the player at the net should play a volley. If the ball is hit with underspin, the ball will probably land long and hence the player at the net should let the ball go.

When positioned at the net and your opponent is attempting a passing shot, there are a number of important points to be considered. While having watched your opponent in previous matches or during the present one, can you say that he prefers to hit cross-court rather than down the line when he is stationary? When he is moving? If your opponent prefers to hit one type of shot from a certain position, protect that area a little bit more and give him more area to hit the shot that he would least prefer to hit. If your opponent hits both cross-court and down-the-line shots, are there certain visual clues that will allow you to determine the direction of the ball?

The body position and the backswing of the stroke may give information as to the *direction of the ball*. Players who hit groundstrokes with an open stance, i.e. not stepping towards the net with the front foot, tend to hit cross-court, a natural movement of the body. Often there are players who have certain idiosyncrasies in their strokes that indicate the type of passing shot, or lob that will be hit. For example, a player may drop his wrist and/or lower his front shoulder if he wishes to hit a cross-court forehand, while he may give a greater shoulder turn if he wants to hit down the line. Some players will open the face of the racquet up before hitting a lob. Such a visual clue, if picked up by an alert net player, should enable him to get in the best possible position for the return.

● Visual clues on returning the serve

The direction and spin of a serve can often be determined in advance by looking and interpreting the visual clues. Watch your opponent's ball toss. If the ball toss is thrown directly over the player's head, the serve will most likely be hit with topspin. If the ball toss is made to the right by a right-handed server, the serve will be a slice. Note your opponent's serving grip. If it is a forehand grip, it will be difficult for the server to hit a slice serve.

The position of the feet will often give information as to the direction of the serve. Often a line drawn from one toe to another will point in the direction that the ball will go. If you see your opponent's back foot is in wide position then the serve will probably be wide. If the server's back foot is positioned down the center, the serve will probably be down the center of the court.

If your opponent takes a stand at a wide angle from the center line of the court, he may be trying for a wide-angled shot. You should shift your position to the angle of an opponent's stance. If your opponent moves ten degrees to the right, then you should make an appropriate and similar change to your right.

If the server bends his knees greatly then the serve will probably kick higher as the server will be hitting up from under the ball. Players who are capable of placing their serve to one corner or the other may look just before they serve to the spot on the court they hope to serve to. If a player can pick up this visual clue, he will certainly have an advantage in preparing for the return.

● Anticipate the speed of the ball, for your stroke depends upon it

Many coaches, books, and magazines frequently will analyze in great detail the proper stroke mechanics without regard to the speed of the ball. There is no such thing as a shot you should absolutely try to make, be it a forehand, or other tennis stroke, because the stroke largely depends upon the time available to complete it.

This is why intermediates run into trouble attempting to improve their game. They take their forty-mile-an-hour strokes and apply them to an eighty-mile-an-hour ball and lose every time. If an intermediate plays against a better player who has a consistent first serve, that player will invariably lose half the games in which he is not serving. To prepare himself for the velocity of ball is accustomed to, he has to back away from his opponent to behind the baseline.

Behind the baseline, many players can play ballet-type tennis with fully developed strokes with a long backswing, a good impact, and an extended follow-through. But put a little heat on that ball and the comfort of that former swing disappears.

The demands of speed require that the whole time frame of the shot must be accelerated. To save seconds, so that there is more time for the stroke, a player must read correctly his opponent's moves. As soon as his opponent's racquet comes across his body, he must start scampering for a cross-court shot. If the ball isn't going too fast, then he may still have time to swing the way he was taught in tennis school. But if the ball is slammed from an overhead smash or serve, he may

Tony Roche is about to put underspin on this shot in close to the net. His swing starts high and will finish low.

arrive at the scene and find he is late for the big action. He has to sacrifice the luxury of putting his racquet all the way back: the backswing must be shortened to the available time. The stroke, as it is shortened, takes an interesting rotation. With a slow ball, the ball is hit level with or slightly ahead of the forward foot. As the swing is shortened, the racquet is brought forward and the hit is made well in front of the body.

If a long backswing is attempted with the fast ball, the player's hit will be late. The abbreviated backswing is the surest way to handle the fast shot.

The need for forward movement on the fast return is not only a matter of stroke economy — it is also the only way to see the ball. The faster the ball is travelling, the larger the zone of fog as it approaches you. So the best recourse is to move toward the area of visual security — where the ball came from.

Perhaps the most cautious return of service is the chip return where the racquet is tilted slightly back to create a little underspin to make the ball rise to insure that it will clear the net.

The only sensible way to deal with speed is to move aggressively into the ball despite the visual handicap of a fast ball. Alex S. was a competent player nurtured on slow stroke lessons but could not adapt to the fast game until he got mad enough to become aggressive. He began to play at age forty and very soon his strokes were good enough that he could hit at the baseline with the better players. He was not a gifted athlete but he was bright, studied the game, and took lessons. And he was determined. He was an unbelievable retriever. He would never relinquish a point if it meant running his guts out for an impossible drive at the other end of the court.

But Alex was getting killed on the serves. And they were killing him. He was not a good loser. He was a terrible loser. His irritability became evident. Even his wife became aware of his irritability after losing a match to players he felt fundamentally superior to. She felt that once he could get past the obstacle of the serve, he had a better chance than ever of winning the point.

His wife finally interceded and she bought him a beautiful

return of service. He was going to learn to deal with speed.

Unfortunately, his lessons were in the slow game, so he couldn't transfer slow-motion strokes to fast-action games. He knew what to do but couldn't do it. He became tangled in the web of tennis analysis.

The lessons were not helping him. They only made him angry. And his anger made him aggressive. He was going to attack the ball come what may.

And he did — to his surprise, his aggressive play worked. As long as he moved forward, taking the chance, he profited. When he lay back, waiting for the ball to slow down so he could follow it, he was late and out of position.

He finally learned how to cope with speed. He did the same on the tennis court as he did in business. He was aggressive and took command. He took the risks to improve himself.

At the age of forty, he did not have the fleetness of foot to become a great player, but his standing definitely improved on the tennis court. He wasn't Alex the Great but for a time he was pleased to be Alex the Good.

Anticipation requires a little more than reading tennis signals. A player must be able to move fast to take advantage of his early information and tailor his strokes to the speed of the ball. Anticipation is the prelude to shotmaking. Without it, a player must be confined to slow tennis or moderate speed tennis played around the baseline.

● Shotmaking

Classical tennis strokes are emphasized in instruction manuals and books on tennis but rarely on the tennis court. There are strokes for the forehand and the backhand but no prototypes are present for the tremendous variety of factors that affect each shot. Is the forehand stroke the same for shoulder-high, waist-high, knee-high, or ankle-high shots? All they really have in common is that they come to the same side — the forehand. Is the forehand the same at twenty, forty, sixty, or eighty miles per hour? Anybody who is used to slow tennis knows they must do something different when the speed is increased. Is the forehand the same off spinners versus flat shots? Is the forehand the same on clay, grass or cement? How can it be — the speed, bounce, and even the auditory signals are different. The forehand shot is certainly different again if you have run into the ball and crowded it or are off-balance when you hit. Some of our best pictures of the professionals show them hitting off-stride and completely disjointed. Tennis shots of the professionals do not always yield classical poses.

Michael Stitt, a member of the Ontario Junior Tennis Team, ranked #8 in Canada for under 14, demonstrates the mechanics of a good stroke while playing a slow ball.

The variables are enormous. What happens if a player arrives at the ball late? If their is a wind? If the floor of the court is uneven and the ball takes an erratic bounce? If the sun is out? Will a train or parade go by? Is the ball fresh? Are all of the balls in the can of even pressure and bounce? Is the racquet strung tightly or loosely? Are the racquet strings gut or nylon? It makes a difference — at least, that is what the tennis analysts and manufacturers tell us. Now if a player on a clay court uses a graphite racquet strung with gut and has to hit a high bounce topspin ball going at sixty miles an hour while rushing to the ball — is that forehand shot going to be different than one hit with a wooden racquet tightly strung with nylon when the ball is moving slowly, taken at the baseline by a player who has two feet on the ground and is swinging below knee-level? The stroke mechanics and body orientation will be quite different for each shot even though they are both on the forehand.

An awkward stance by John Newcombe. One foot is stable, the knees are bent, and the ball is about to be hit in front of the fog zone. Looks clumsy, but all the ingredients of a good stroke are here.

So there is no such thing as perfect strokes or perfect tennis players because even the best players do not do the same thing all the time. The great ones hit differently because they move differently and see the ball differently. How can one standardize where in the flight of the ball a player should abandon trying to follow it into the racquet? Some players can definitely follow the ball longer than others. Others are obsessed with trying because if has been drilled into their heads until they have a headache.

Some coaches are very mechanistic and tell you what to do with your arms and legs in detailed sequence as the tennis stroke evolves. Others are totally amorphous and tell you to relax, to copy from your visual memory of tennis strokes and play the game without being conscious of what you do. Certainly the best tennis players have coaches so the game is just not completely flabby or structureless. There are patterns and approaches to balls but no orthodox body motions. We feel that somewhere between the analytical and synthetic approaches to tennis is perhaps the best approach to learning the game. It is not possible to learn totally by osmosis, diffusion, meditation the visual principles that govern the game —the eye is a limited organ and our appreciation of its limitations are profound. But we have to know how to approach the ball before hitting it. We have taken the visual approach to shotmaking. Our emphasis is on relating to the stroke to the kind of shot coming toward you — fast, straight, bouncing high or low — whether it's coming straight or off to the side. The only time you may have the semblance of a standard stroke is by playing against a ball machine, where automated balls spew out at the same pace to the same place. Learning by example can get a player started, and perhaps advance that person to the intermediate ranks. But one can get hooked into a level of performance without some insight into the dynamics of the game and will only slowly improve. Also, a player must know his own idiosyncrasies — those which are tolerated and beneficial and those which are counter-productive.

● Groundstrokes The forehand

The forehand is the most easily learned of all the tennis strokes. In all probability, the cave man with his club used a primitive forehand to destroy marauding animals. (He may even have let out a fierce grunt just like Jimmy Connors in doing so.) The forehand is the basic swing of baseball batters, and golfers, and even boxers hit forehand. So beginners take to the forehand and find some comfort and security in the swing. As their game progresses, the backhand is acquired and, for a silent few even preferred, but for most players, especially non-professionals, the forehand remains the people's choice.

If you are right-handed, the forehand may be an easier stroke to perfect if your left eye is dominant. Eye dominance is based upon your having a "better seeing" eye whereas "handedness" is based upon cerebral or brain dominance which, in a right-handed person, means a left-sided cerebral dominance. Suffice it to say because you are right-handed does not mean you must be right-eyed.

Now if you're playing slow tennis or hitting at the baseline when the height of the ball is relatively low and velocity just enough to keep the ball floating in air, you can use a classic or standard forehand tennis stroke.

The racquet is held in the Eastern grip which is simply accomplished by shaking hands with the racquet. The palm of

Connors and Tracey Austin with forehand strokes. Connors hits on the run; Austin has one foot firmly planted for a more accurate and hard return.

the hand should be placed on the inside edge of the racquet with the thumb and forefinger separated to make a V.

As soon as the ball is seen coming to your forehand side,

turn the shoulders and hips to the side and take your racquet back. Ideally, your racquet should be pointing almost directly at the back fence prior to hitting the ball. Once this is done, the movement is strictly forward and the player steps forward to meet the ball. A transfer of weight should occur from the back to front foot. When the shot is completed all your weight should be on your front foot. Arthur Ashe, in his tennis clinics, points out "your objective should be to keep the ball on the strings for as much of that hitting zone as possible — by hitting smoothly through the ball, as the pros say. The longer you can keep the ball on the strings, the more control you will have over your shot. So you should really concentrate on the ball in the hitting zone. You must try to watch it intently, although it is unlikely that you will be able to see the actual contact."

Even in slow tennis, we agree that you will not see the ball hit the strings of the racquet. The impact time is far too short to witness it so, if you can, concentrate on a smooth stroke.

The follow-through should occur after impact so that the racquet is carried forward. The racquet should end up high in front of the body, be vertical in orientation, and be pointing in the direction you want the ball to go.

A good shot will be made under the following conditions:

1) Your racquet is held firmly in the palm of your hand. This is to prevent the racquet face from inclining upon impact with the ball.
2) The racquet is vertical at impact to insure the ball is returned directly and that the ball hits the sweet spot.
3) You keep your body low through the entire motion of the stroke. If you move to an upright position before completing the stroke, this may cause the ball to rise sharply and send the shot long.

● Backhand

The differences between the forehand and backhand are not that great when one approaches the game from the point of view of the receiver. On the backhand side, a player still has to contend with a variety of bounce patterns, ball speeds, and spins. A player has to be aware of the visual vagaries of running and be able to reach the ball with motion at least partially halted.

Some of the top professionals love the backhand and the mental picture of Jimmy Connors in play invariably evokes his image hitting his two-handed backhand shot with intensity and energy. The beginners and intermediates do not relish the backhand. They find it awkward to stroke and a shot that cannot easily be executed with terrific power.

The motions of a good backhand swing have similar ingredients to the forehand. The best groundstrokes are

Connors moves into the ball with his two-handed backhand and hits with considerable power. Unlike Borg, Connors was not able to follow the ball close to the point of impact.

accomplished if you are not moving, and are situated at the baseline to receive balls with declining velocity.

The racquet should be taken back quickly but smoothly, cradled in your non-racquet hand. The grip should be altered to the backhand grip which requires a one-half turn of rotation from the forehand grip so that the forefinger's knuckle is on top. In this way your wrist will be behind the hitting face of the racquet. The racquet head should point to the back fence, with the body sideways to the oncoming ball. The racquet is then swung forward from the shoulder in a fluid motion as the body weight is shifted from the back foot to the front foot. A smooth follow-through is important and

Borg makes a two-handed backhand shot while the ball is in front of his body.

the racquet face should point in the direction you wish the ball to go.

It is usually advantageous to make contact with the ball in front of your body. Backhand shots make impact at least six inches in front of a typical forehand shot. The ball can be hit further in front of the body by getting down to the ball by bending your knees.

Very popular today is the two-handed backhand. It is the choice for Chris Evert and Bjorn Borg. It has much appeal as it is easier to teach young children and aid players who suffer from tennis elbow. But it is more than a therapeutic stroke as it is easier to generate topspin and power with this stroke. There are some drawbacks to the two-handed approach. It limits one's reach which may be important on a running backhand. It is also not as flexible as it makes hitting high and low balls more difficult.

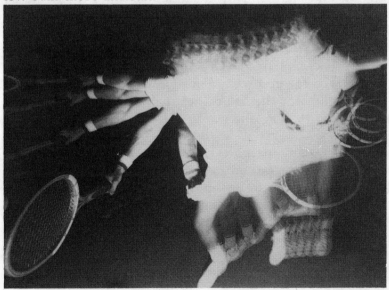

A strobe analysis of the backhand as displayed by Ray Stein. During the sequence the eyes and head are never turned to the ball. (Jordan Slatt)

On slow shots, the visual patterns are interesting to observe. The eyes or head, sometimes both, are turned in the direction of the ball almost to impact. The player hits the ball somewhat like a golfer, with the eyes down on the ball but does not see where his own ball goes. The ball can be followed close to impact, and the player uses his visual memory to place the shot.

On high velocity shots, the eyes are usually forward and not on the ball so the player doesn't look at and actually cannot see any of the action close to his racquet. One of the problems in the high velocity backhand is that the ball must be contacted far out in front of the body in order to cut down on the visual guesstimates and to generate more power.

● Hitting on the run

Of course, when you run for the ball your visual acuity decreases and worsens the faster you go. So, if you are sprinting for a laterally placed shot, you will have difficulty reading the ball in space. Before you hit, plant one foot to steady your head and eyes. This will also stop your sideways motion and allow you to make a stroke which should be vertical or perpendicular to the net.

A good groundstroke while hitting on the run will be made if:
1) You take your racquet back before or while running so that you are prepared to make the hit;
2) You glide for the ball rather than sprint because a fluid running motion is less apt to affect the stability of your vision;
3) You stop running with your weight on the back foot so the front foot can be correctly positioned to meet the ball;
4) You anticipate your opponent's shot and move the moment he hits allowing yourself time to position for the return. Stability increases the chance of a successful return.

● The high bounce and how to control it

Topspin has become fashionable in modern play because the shot will easily clear the net and the topspin will give the ball added life at the bounce. The higher the bounce of the ball the more difficult it is to play. High arching lobs are tougher to play than the low lob shots. High bouncing balls are a much greater problem than low bouncing balls because of the loss of valuable ground clues which happens when a ball is much above eye level — players need the ground for orientation.

A high bouncing shot is difficult to return because most players lack the ability to generate power on groundstrokes hit at shoulder level — especially on the backhand side. Furthermore, the execution of the stroke is so different from a regular tennis stroke that it is difficult to become proficient at the shot. There is always the danger of coming down too abruptly and hitting the ball into the net. It is generally best to return the high bouncing balls back high over the net. To prevent the ball from sailing out of bounds, a good topspin is essential. The topspin placed on the ball enables one to hit the ball with a good margin of safety over the net and still have it land within the court. Although it seems like a miserable thing to point out, the high bouncing ball with topspin is especially effective against short players.

Arthur Ashe returns a high bouncing spinner with underspin. His racquet makes contact with the ball as it descends from a high to low position augmenting the existing spin on the ball.

● Playing the low bounce

People spend most of their lives looking ahead at eye level or peering below so they are most comfortable looking down.

Man is basically a downcast animal. It reflects in his tennis play. Those balls that bounce low at knee-level or waist-high are easiest to judge in space: there are vivid reference points such as the markings on the court surface and the proximity of the net.

Playing the low ball at the baseline is a straightforward stroke. The velocity of the ball is slow enough that the eyes can follow the ball to within a yard or two of the point of impact. Provided the racquet is held back in readiness for the shot, the knees are bent and the player is positioned sideways to the ball and is moving forward into the shot, the player is prepared to make a successful stroke.

Hitting from the baseline means that the ball need not be steeply hit to clear the net. Flat shots, spins, or topspins offer a reasonable choice of shots that will clear the net.

It is only when the ball is low and the net close by, such as occurs when the ball lands in the front court, that special adjustments to the stroke must be made. The angle of the rise of the ball must be greater to allow the ball to clear the net. This means that the racquet must be held lower than usual. However, when making a short shot the player should avoid the temptation of dropping the head of the racquet and shovelling the ball. The ball will not only clear the net but frequently the other court as well. Such returns become either set-ups or long shots.

Again, early preparation is important so that the ball is not hit on the run and the racquet outstretched to reach the ball. A low stance and a controlled swing are important in assuring that the ball clears the net and lands safely in the opponent's court.

 ## Some suggestions for hitting the ground-stroke

The topspin groundstroke is favoured because it is a relatively safe stroke and the ball will bounce high with a lot of speed so that the opponent will have difficulty judging the ball and making his stroke.

Anticipate early and glide to the shot. A running dash will

suppress vision. Hit the ball in front of the advanced foot but do not try to follow the ball into the racquet. Make a controlled stroke with a follow-through keeping in mind how high the ball must be played to clear the net.

Some of the factors that will determine the stroke of your forehand or backhand are how high the ball is bouncing, whether it is fast or slow, and what kind of spin is on the ball. There are other variables such as wind, sun, and court surface which will also affect the stroke and these will be discussed later.

● The serve

The serve is the only shot in tennis at which a player has complete control over the ball. It can be an explosive shot that can rip a tennis game apart. A player's reputation can rest on the serve alone. If it is going well for him, he is considered to have the game in hand. Thought is rarely given to the opponent who returns the serve. Very few players are heralded by their return of service because few players can return a hot serve with an offensive reply. Most players either hit it defensively or are very inconsistent in their replies. The serve is the single shot in tennis that can win the most points. So tough are the elements of a serve, that it is considered a coup for a player to break his opponent's service.

What is so awesome about the serve? In top-ranking tennis, the speed of the ball exceeds the abilities of the eye. For years, coaches have maintained that following the serve is possible. "Keep your eye on the ball" seemed to be a maxim that would solve the sensory problems of tennis. It is a good thing the tennis racquet is the size of a small wastebasket, otherwise players would miss the ball entirely.

A good professional hitting a fast serve might connect sixty to seventy percent of the time. Pancho Gonzalez made tennis history by connecting seventy-five percent of the time. A good club player, if he is delivering his fast and mighty best, would do well to achieve a hot delivery forty percent of the time. But the statistics are really shattering when you consider the number of times a good serve is returned with both power and direction.

Of course, the inferiority of the human eye as a visual guide is not the only reason players return fast serves with the energy of a stone wall. The time allowed for the motions of a good return is insufficient for the demands of the stroke. Everything speeds up like an old Charlie Chaplin movie so that movements seem jerky and incomplete. Unless a player has quick anticipation, fleetness of foot, and a very rapid arm motion, he can never make a solid stroke on the return of serve. What usually results is a block, punch, or half a forehand — some piece of a forehand but never the whole thing.

The serve is a controlled overhand smash. It has none of the drawbacks of an overhead smash as the height the ball is tossed is minimal, and the player can insure that his body is properly placed for the hit. Although the serve is made from the baseline, the easy orientation of the ball to player makes the serve an easier task than smashing a high lob. The ball is tossed three to four feet above the head, comfortably within the field of vision.

Most players could easily get most of their serves in the opponent's court if they were allowed the entire court. The drawback to the serve is that it must be directed to the front service court which is only 13.5' wide and 21' deep. Normally a player behind the baseline wouldn't attempt such a short shot because it is difficult and quite improbable that it can be made with any speed on the ball. This drawback is an advantage if the serve goes in, because the server can displace his opponent sharply with shots that are required to land in the anterior service court. The two favourite targets for the serve are deep and wide to the forehand side so the player has to run out of bounds and out of position to reach the ball, and one directed to the player's backhand side. The displacement shot to the forehand is difficult to return because it demands the opponent move to reach a ball angled away from him. As we discussed before, body movement is synonymous with visual instability. The backhand is also a trying shot because it must be hit in front of the body which is not easy on a blistering serve.

● The basic mechanics of the serve are as follows:

● Ready Position

Stand tall with your front foot at a 45° angle to the baseline and your back foot parallel to the baseline and at least shoulder width apart. A line drawn from the back toe to the front toe should point to the court you are serving to.

● Ball Toss

The ball should be held softly in the fingertips and released at full stretch above your head. Try to throw the ball in the natural path of the racquet, which is slightly to the right (if right-handed) and out in front (the taller you are the further out in front you can throw the ball). If you release the ball above your head and hit it with a fully extended racquet arm, you need only throw the ball up the length of the racquet, which is about twenty-seven inches.

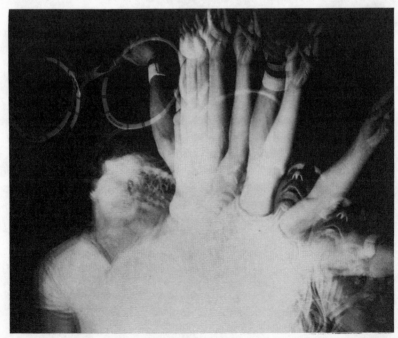

The ball toss and serve — the head and eyes turned upward to see the ball enter the field of vision on the toss and subsequent stroke.

Stroke

With both arms out in front at the start, they drop down together. After moving down together the arms separate. The tossing arm moves smoothly upward and releases the ball. At the same time, the hitting arm swings with the motion of throwing a ball.

Keep the hitting elbow high and bent as you "wind up" to the shoulder. In the "shoulder" position you should be able to "scratch your back" with the head of the racquet. From the shoulder, the racquet head is "thrown" upwards at the ball. The hitting arm extends, reaches high, and allows the racquet to hit up and over the ball. Continue through the swing and follow-through across your body. The back foot should step easily into the court.

There are three different types of serves, each being a slight variation on the basic serve. They are the flat serve, the spin serve, and the American twist.

● The flat serve

The flat serve is hit with an open-faced racquet. The ball is tossed directly in front of the body and, if it were not hit, it would land about one and one-half feet in front of the server.

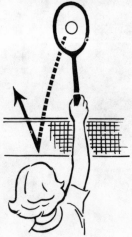

Flat serve: The racquet face is flat to the ball which will produce no spin. The ball will bounce directly forward after the bounce.

The serve is driven by the power of the wrist. The wrist snaps forward from its cocked position as the arm carries over the head with the forward motion of the body. The momentum applied to the flat serve comes from the forward movement of the arm, the snap of the wrist, and the thrust of the body hinged at the feet. After the ball has been struck the body should be tilted well into the court with the shoulders

Martina Navaratilova stretches to obtain full power on her serve. Once contact has been made she looks to her opponent's court.

relatively straight and the racquet hand brought down across the body in a smooth complete follow-through.

The risk-reward ratio of the flat serve is high because the ball's flat trajectory means that the margin of error is not greater than a few inches. However, if it doesn't almost skim the net, the ball will go long. It is difficult to consistently skim the net since one aims entirely from visual memory. The ball toss of the serve is one time a player must keep his eye on the ball. For this security, he must give up visually aiming. He doesn't see the court into which he is trying to place the ball. Many players study the court before the serve to imprint the target on their brain to aid in service direction.

The only good thing about receiving a flat or cannonball serve is that the ball continues in a straight line after the bounce. This should be anticipated.

The flat serve is invariably the first serve because it is a powerfully delivered shot. The racquet follows straight behind the ball after impact. Frequently there may be a little slice added to the flat serve so that the racquet strikes the ball going from left to right. Basically it is a direct shot. The player returning the serve should learn to recognize the motion of the flat serve because, if the ball has any power, he will not be in a good position to compensate for a veer to the right or left. Once he knows it is flat, he will be able to anticipate the straight trajectory of the ball. At top speeds, the only chance a player has to break service is early anticipation.

● The slice serve

Every tennis player should have a slice serve in his repertoire. It is the best form of insurance a tennis player has. A good club player only has a fifty percent chance of safely serving cannonballs each time which means if he double blasts the serve, he will double fault one in four.

The slice serve has some speed, a little spin and a tendency to veer to one side after the bounce. It can be hit so that it safely clears the net and yet will drop down to the service court with a good margin of safety.

The ball toss and the movement of the racquet arm are identical to that of the flat serve; the only difference lies in the action of the wrist which, instead of bringing the racquet straight through the ball, causes the face of the racquet to move from left to right across the back of the ball. The ball is hit ahead of the body with the body and arm outstretched. The follow-through should be smooth so that the racquet ends up on the side opposite to your hitting arm.

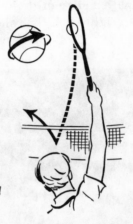

Slice serve: The racquet face meets the ball at an angle of about 45 degrees. The ball will veer to the left after the bounce.

Visually, the slice serve is difficult to track. The kick to the side by the ball hampers anticipation and the speed of the ball is a little too fast to allow the eye to watch it all the way to the racquet. Many players can return a slice serve, but often they do not do it with precision or power as the ball is apt to veer off from its straight trajectory and hit the racquet outside the sweet spot. Unless, one anticipates the exact deflection of the bounce and prepares for it, the return of serve will require some last minute stretching on the part of the player.

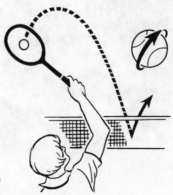

Twist serve: The racquet face brushes across the back of the ball from left to right. The ball will veer to the right after the bounce.

American twist serve

This serve is the most awkward and difficult to execute of all the services. It belongs to the arsenal of the advanced player with extremely flexible joints and wrists. With the American twist serve the ball is tossed overhead and slightly to the left and the ball is hit with a snap of the wrist as the arm moves directly from left to right with the follow-through finishing on the same side of the body as the serving arm instead of the opposite side.

American twist serve — Paul Ramirez serves with the American twist. The arm and racquet wind up on the same side of the body. Brian Gottfried is at the net.

The visual clue for the return of service is that the ball is tossed almost directly behind the server's head. An extreme degree of back flex is needed to get the racquet behind the ball.

Visually the ball takes a confusing course. The service action is from right to left in the air but reverses on the bounce and goes from left to right to one's opponent's backhand.

The twist serve requires an elbow and wrist snap. It should be avoided by any player with tennis elbow problems or a bad back. It causes and aggravates both conditions. This service, because it is difficult to master, is often the last to be learned.

● Return of serve

● Ready position

Start in a good waiting position. Face the opponent and be ready to move. Adjust your position according to the server: if he serves wide, shift wide; if he serves hard and flat, move back; if he serves slowly or with a spin, move forward.

● Preparation

When the direction and type of serve is determined, turn to the appropriate side and take your racquet back with a shortened backswing.

● Hit

Contact should be made in front of your body, with your front foot and weight coming forward with the swing.

● Follow-through

The hitting arm is extended shoulder high, pointing in the direction you wish the ball to go.

● Important points to remember on return of serve:

1) Do not attempt a full swing on a return of serve. The sequence is too rapid to allow it. Either block the shot

using the speed of the ball to generate its return or use an abbreviated backswing.

2) Move forward into the ball. This accomplishes three things: It moves you out of zone of fog, it allows you to cut down the angle of the serve, and more power is generated in your stroke you bring your body forward.

3) Anticipate by reading your opponent's signals. You may not see much after the bounce. A flat serve bounces straight. A slice serve deflects to the right of the receiver. The American twist serve deflects to the left of the receiver.

4) Deal with the return of serve realistically. If you are capable of playing an aggressive return of serve, stand inside the baseline so that you make early contact with the ball. If you are uncomfortable with speed, move back and let the ball slow down.

The flat serve can be played farther back on the court to allow the ball to lose some of its pace. Although the speed of the ball is slower behind the baseline, the displacement of the ball from the court is greater. With a spin serve, retreat to the back court is fraught with danger as the ball will move farther away from you, the farther you are behind the baseline. Older players, unfit players, and slow players who are lead-footed but sharp-eyed, should play the flat serve as far back as possible as speed can be tamed if the ball travels far enough. Young strong athletes prefer to deal directly with the speed of the ball by standing as close into the court as possible, which with their fast reflexes enables them to take fewer steps to get to the ball.

The major differences between receiving the ball deep and intercepting it closer to the bounce is the length of visual hold on the ball. The farther back you go, the longer you can track the path of the ball. The ball can be hit at the level of the advancing foot and there may be time for a more complete swing.

Women seem to be able to watch a tennis ball on return of service longer than men. The women photographed during professional matches, including Chris Evert and Billie Jean

King, appeared to keep their eye on the ball till late. Their eyes and head were definitely turned toward the ball during random pictures and fast sequences. It is quite possible that there was some visual miss between the eye and the ball, but since we were using photography as a guide we couldn't be sure. There are methods of electronically monitoring eye position and visual gaze, but we preferred to make our judgements on tournament and ordinary play rather than head for the laboratory. It may be argued convincingly that women in professional play deal with a slower ball on the serve. Physiologically, of course, there is no difference in eye function or visual activity between the sexes. Since the tracking ability between men and women are the same, the apparent differences must be in the slightly slower game played by women.

In men's play, the discrepancy between the position of the eyes and that of the ball is enormous. Players like Connors, Nastase, Dibbs, McEnroe, Vilas, and Gerulaitis seemed to be playing blind. Their eyes were straight ahead when the ball was at their side, almost to the racquet. Young expert male amateurs and local professionals showed the same results. It was evident that they did not attempt to follow the ball, but rather moved into the ball's trajectory. Despite the speed, some top professionals like Jimmy Connors could even manage a full swing on a fast return of service.

5) Vary your returns whenever possible. Hit cross-court, down the middle, down the line, lob. Drop over the net, drive the ball to his toes — do anything and everything except execute the same return all the time. Don't give your opponent the game by letting him know that you always return consistently cross-court, down the line, or down the middle.

● The volley

A volley is any return that is hit before the ball bounces.

There are two basic visual problems with the volley. Running to gain control at the net really suppresses a player's

Ilie Nastase: The ball is hit in front of his body.

vision. Hitting a ball close to the net and before the bounce means playing a tennis ball at its greatest velocity. The ball must be hit in front of the body because it is difficult to judge the ball if it is about to go by you.

At the net, the entire stroke is amputated because of the speed of the ball and there is usually only enough time to block or punch the ball. If the ball is fast, the power of the ball is sufficient to propel its own return. If the ball is slow, then a punching motion with a short follow-through can be used.

The volley is one of the most visually demanding shots in tennis. Early anticipation is the key which means you must see your opponent hit the ball. Your body motion must be still for an instance to enable you to see your opponent and his moves.

You must not be in motion when you hit the ball, as your visual judgement will be greatly compromised. Contact must be made in front of your body. You move your racquet into the direction that the ball is coming from. Do not attempt to follow the ball into the racquet.

The speed of the ball demands readiness. Stay on the balls of your feet, ready to spring forward to attack the ball, and

Brian Gottfried is off-balance as he attempts a shoulder-high volley; he does not try to follow the ball.

keep the racquet head high by supporting it at the throat with the non-hitting hand.

On low balls, bend the knees and take a large step forward with the front foot. Don't drop the racquet head below your wrist.

The backhand volley should be the easier to hit because the racquet is carried across the body forcing you to hit in front. Most club players volley poorly from the backhand because they don't anticipate early enough and are not accustomed to hitting in front of the body. They develop poor visual habits from their forehand side which does not serve them well on the more critical backhand side.

Gerulaitis plays a backhand volley in front of his body. He is not attempting a visual hold on the ball.

The half volley

The half volley is hit just after the bounce and very close to the ground. It is a pick-up shot that a player is forced to make when the ball is aimed at his feet or when he is caught in motion and can't cover the distance to make the volley shot.

The half volley is played according to computed trajectory of the ball. It is played off a low bouncing shot that is best returned with the player almost parallel to the flight of the

Billy Jean King bends her knees to play a low half volley.

ball, the knees bent to carry the body low, and with the racquet moving from a low to a high position so as to lift the ball over the net. The follow-through should finish high and point in the direction you wish the ball to go. Your success with this shot will vary with your dynamic visual acuity, your anticipation, and how fast you move.

Although the half volley is usually played by the player at the net or in the mid-court area, it can also be hit from the baseline. By hitting a half volley from the baseline, it speeds up the tempo of the game and gives your opponent less time to react to your shot. It is commonly employed by the advanced player against an opponent coming to or at the net so as to throw him off-balance.

Virginia Wade is caught in a difficult position at the net and she is forced to play a half volley.

● The drop shot

A drop shot is one which lands in the service court preferably close to the net. There are two major advantages to this shot. A player has to run to reach it so his visual control of the ball is poor. The return shot is invariably a weak reply since the net must be cleared from a position quite close to it.

The best drop shots are those in which you are close to the net and your opponent is behind the baseline. It is difficult to gauge the velocity of the ball required to carry it over the net, so the closer to the net you are, the better the chance of a safe hit. The farther your opponent is from the net, the greater the distance and the faster he must run to reach the ball. Many players don't gauge the ball properly and either run into it or stop short and have to reach to scrape the ball off the ground.

The best drop shots are the ones that catch your opponent unprepared. To mask the shot, take the racquet back as though a regular slice forehand or backhand is attempted. A full swing is employed: bring the racquet from a high to low position to create a little underspin. The motion should be soft, smooth, and continuous with a pushing and lifting motion that elevates the ball. If the ball is hit well, it will go over the net by a safe margin and then simply "die". If the shot is well disguised, one's opponent will not realize the difference in the ball's flight until it is too late. It is best to err on the side of too much power as opposed to too little. If the ball drops on your side of the net, you simply lose the point.

The drop shot is an adjunct to basic tennis strokes. Very few players climb to great heights on the drop shot alone. Chris Evert employs it to complement her deep ground-strokes. She waits for the opportunity to hit a drop shot which occurs when her opponent hits a ball into mid-court. She employs her drop shot to bring her opponent up and then makes a winning pass shot or lob from her opponent's weak reply.

● A few pearls on drop shots

Do not attempt the drop shot on any ball with a lot of speed on it. You will not be able to brake your shot. In all probability you won't even see the ball.

The return of a drop shot is made under the worst visual conditions. The player must run almost half a court, hit the ball while in motion, and hit from below upwards at an awkward angle to allow the ball to clear the net. The best return is one that allows you to survive. Don't do too much with it. A lob, a placement, another drop, anything that goes over the net is good. Sluggers don't earn their reputation from drop shots.

The drop shot is a mixer. It changes the pace of the game, upsets rigid players with stereotyped motor responses, and can tax the energies of the unfit players causing visual as well as muscular fatigue.

The drop shot is best on clay or synthetic court surfaces when the ball "dies" quickly. On cement, the ball is carried to the player because of the better bounce and the value of the shot is diminished.

The follow-through of the drop shot should be in the direction that the ball is intended to go. It is called aiming and you do it with your racquet — not your eye. We saw a master dart performer show this aiming the arm rather graphically. He threw several darts in a cluster on target. He then proceeded to do it with eyes closed. Your follow-through is the sighting device of your racquet.

A drop shot should be hit down the line — not cross-court. The down-the-line shot travels a shorter distance, and hence the ball remains in the air for a shorter period of time, which results in less time for the opponent to respond.

 ## The best antidote to a drop shot

Move forward the instant you recognize the drop shot. The solution is not in running fast which ruins your visual hold on the ball, but in anticipation and starting fast. The fast start will allow a smoother running motion, preserving your visual hold on your opponent.

The lob

The lob can be an exceptionally effective weapon if hit with control, and there are many times during the course of play when it is the best shot to use. Certain advantages of the stroke are obvious. It allows the hitter time to recover and can move opponents back from the net. It is used as a tactical stroke although some players employ it as a regular shot. In addition, the lob can serve as an approach shot or return of serve and, with its element of surprise, can often win the point outright.

1) Use the basic forehand and backhand-style grips to hit the forehand and backhand lobs. When executing the stroke, the face of the racquet should be tilted slightly back.
2) Once in position, step forward toward the ball and, using the basic low to high pattern of swing, hit the underside of the ball. Accentuate the upward motion of the swing for good elevation on the shot.
3) Since the lob must be controlled, try to hold or "carry" the ball on the strings as you redirect its path upward.
4) Complete the stroke with a high follow-through.

● Specific lob points to remember

1) Plan the trajectory of the lob so that the apex — "peak" — of the shot is directly above the player at the net.
2) The lob should generally be hit with slight underspin for control.
3) When hitting the lob emphasize height and depth. Lob for a spot near the baseline, preferably on the backhand side.
4) Hit harder and higher when lobbing against the wind. Use more backspin when lobbing with the wind.
5) Avoid standing and watching the lob, hoping that it will drop in. Always assume your opponent will return every ball you hit.
6) Remember that a cross-court lob can travel a greater distance than one hit down the line.

● The visual side of the lob

Next to the very fast service, the lob is the most taxing shot to track in space. Some of the material we have covered in the section on depth perception, so we shall concentrate on the practical points of lobbing.

High lobs are more difficult to track than low lobs because a player has to rely completely on depth perception, must concentrate a longer time with his small pupils (pupils constrict as they look up at the sun or overhead lights which changes the depth of focus), and gauge the acceleration of the dropping ball which increases as the ball falls. Most tennis balls get slower as they come to you — only lobs get faster. The best antidote to a high lob, for a person with poor depth perception, is to let the ball bounce.

Lobs to the baseline are particularly poisonous because a player must run to reach the ball and at the same time watch the ball. As we have said before, the two arts do not mix too well. Also the further back from the net that the high ball is returned, the greater the chances of error being made and the ball catapulted into the net.

The offensive lob is tactically an effective shot if well disguised. The stroke is usually hit with topspin and aimed so that it travels just over the outstretched player at the net. The ball has a low arch, drops fast, and then takes off because of the topspin. It is a shot that is best left to the advanced player because it is difficult to execute.

Lobs to the backhand side are more troublesome. The player is forced to cross over his own body with his arm and racquet from right to left to hit a ball dropping in space. The cross over is an added burden to hand-eye coordination. A good solution is to avoid this shot altogether, by taking an extra couple of steps so as to play it as a forehand smash.

● The overhead smash

The overhead smash is very similar to the serve. The main differences are that your opponent puts the ball up in the air and can select the court position where he wants to place the ball. It is easier than the serve in that you hit your overhead closer to the net and you have the whole court to hit into. It is more difficult than the serve in that you have to hit a ball that is dropping down fast as opposed to one that is practically motionless (on the serve the ball should hit at the top of the throw). Your first goals should be control and accuracy. You do not have to "smash" every overhead — depth, angle, or placement will also win the point.

A missed overhead smash is the most emotional shot in tennis. It seems so easy to hit a smash and yet among non-tournament players, it is often hit out of the court or into the net with the same frequency as a first serve. It is the kind of error that causes normally conservative men to shout four-letter words, throw their racquets, look plaintively at the sides as though begging for forgiveness from any onlookers, and disrupt the control of their game. Where a player does it in doubles, it makes him want to crawl under one of the tennis lines.

The overhead smash: Sometimes it is difficult to gauge the flight of the ball to put the body under it. Backward reach reduces power and increases the chance of hitting on the racquet edge.

The overhead smash is hit like a serve. Wrist snap adds power. The eyes should be able to follow the ball.

The overhead smash is one of the most difficult shots to make in tennis. There are no easy answers to placing your body under the ball and then hitting an accelerating tennis ball. Here are some considerations to the smash to make it more consistent:

1) As soon as the lob is hit get your racquet down your back and point at the ball with your non-hitting hand. It is not important whether you take a full service swing or an abbreviated one, so long as the racquet drops down your back as early as possible. By pointing at the ball with your non-hitting hand, it makes you watch the ball, turns you sideways to the net and puts most of your weight on your

Jump smash: Navaratilova's racquet is ready but there is no visual control. Strictly for the experts.

back foot. From the shoulder position the racquet's pattern of swing is like the serve. Throw the racquet head up toward the ball, reach high for contact, hit over and through the ball, and finish across your body. Transfer your weight forward as you hit. Your back foot should come naturally forward.

2) The ideal smash is one that is hit with the ball in the same place as if you had tossed it there for a serve.

3) Keep your eye on the ball — it is slow moving and within the capacity of the visual following mechanism. Some players have a terrible habit of closing their eyes before they make contact with the ball.

4) If the ball is lobbed over your backhand side, try if possible to get over and play it as a forehand smash.

5) The jump overhead smash with a scissors kick is strictly for experts. It is for the player who can correctly place his body under the ball and accurately gauge its descent. When such a player jumps in space to aggressively hit the ball, he loses all visual control. His timing must be accurate. He also must have great experience in hitting overhead smashes because if he jumps too early and is forced to hit a ball well in front of his body, the ball will probably travel into the net while, on the other hand, if he jumps too late, and plays a ball that has travelled too far behind his body, the ball will be hit out, unless he makes a fine adjustment at the last second by using wrist action to bring the ball down into the court.

6) If you have no depth perception because of a lazy eye or whatever, then it is safer to allow the lob to bounce and take the shot when it is lower and slower. If your vision is not equally sharp in each eye, you will not possess good depth perception.

PART TWO

Interviews

4 An Interview with Robert Bedard

Robert Bedard was born in St. Hyacinthe, Quebec. He was ranked number one in Canada for eleven years, from 1955 to 1965 inclusive. He was a three-time winner of the Canadian Open Championship for singles and three times for doubles. He received a silver medal at the Pan Am games in Chicago in 1959 and a gold medal in the Canada games in Halifax in 1969. He has been the victor over the number one ranking player in fourteen different countries around the world including the United States, England, France, India, Germany, Belgium, Brazil, Mexico, Sweden, Denmark, Australia, and Italy.

Mr. Bedard has received a B.A. degree and a Bachelor of Education degree from McGill University in Montreal, Canada, and is presently assistant Headmaster at St. Andrew's College, Aurora.

● The interview

Question: You played on the International Tennis Circuit in the 1950s. Since this time tennis has undergone a dramatic increase in popularity and has mushroomed all over the world. What factors may account for the increased popularity of the game?

Answer: Over the years there has been a dramatic decline in the hours of the working man so that he has much more time for leisure activities. This is combined with the fact that there has been greater emphasis on physical fitness. Tennis lends itself both as a body conditioner as well as a social sport. As a result of this there has been a considerable increase in the number of available tennis courts, both indoors and outdoors. In addition the rapid expansion in tournament tennis combined with television coverage of major tournament events has made the average individual more aware of this particular sport. Tennis lends itself well to television and consequently it is brought into the average man's household so that the young as well as the old can watch professionals play.

This game is also one that can appeal to the very young, the elderly, to both men and women and consequently everyone can play at his own level.

Q: How important do you think vision is in the game of tennis?

A: I think vision is very important in the game of tennis particularly at the net or if you are playing against a hard hitter. Actually the important factor, and this applies mainly to doubles, is seeing behind you. It has to do with peripheral vision because you've got to know the trajectory of the ball your partner has just hit even though you are facing the other court. In that way peripheral vision is very important.

You might be in a position where you won't be facing the net, you are running back, you are running for a lob backwards, or you know that you have to see the opponent while you are still running back . . . you have to see what he is doing. That is peripheral vision again. That is the important part.

Q: When you are running for the ball, do you think you can actually identify where your opponent is?

A: Yes, you have to have a good idea. You get fooled once in a while but that is because you haven't concentrated enough. You must see the movement of the opponent.

Q: So if you are attempting a passing shot you can see where your opponent is going?

A: You are definitely going to have some idea of what the opponent is going to try and do and although you are watching the ball you still have to know what is happening on the other side of the net.

Q: Do you think you might use memory — once you go for the ball — to remember where he was standing before?

A: Well, that won't do much good when he moves.

Q: So you think that you might be able to spot him as you are running.

A: Yes.

Q: When do you think you see the ball on the court?

A: When the opposing player is serving you must watch his racquet. Usually, we look at the ball, but looking at the ball means not when it's near the net, but when it is on the opponent's racquet. Then you probably will have one or two steps advantage over the other fellow who doesn't do it that way. If you realize that you are not returning well and the opponent is serving too well for you, all you have to do is watch when he serves; you see the angle of the racquet, you don't see the ball all the way through, but just as the ball has struck his racquet you have made your move. You know where to go for the ball and that's half the battle right there . . . to get into position. The other half is to keep on watching after he has struck the ball. If a person doesn't have particularly good vision, I don't know if he can see the striking movement of the racquet as the opponent is hitting but again that can translate as anticipation. Anticipation doesn't come first, I think that comes second.

Q: So you are seeing the ball not as it comes over the net, but as it's leaving the racquet?

A: Yes, as it's leaving the racquet. Also you must watch the position of the feet, the position of the body. In that way vision is extremely important.

Q: When you make a shot, can you see the ball hit the strings?

A: Not really. I see it on the backhand much better. On the forehand, I find it very difficult possibly because my arm has to come across my body at which point it blocks my vision.

Q: Do you suppose you might lose sight of the ball at least ten feet in front of you rather than at the head of the racquet?

A: I think that is possible. If you concentrate totally you will see even the markings on the ball or the curves, what do you call it —the linings, the seams.* However, it may be that you are not seeing the positive hitting but you think you are. There is no question that when you watch the ball closely as it is almost at you, you are going to hit the ball in the center of the racquet.

Q: Do you actually think you see the ball hit the center of your racquet?

A: I couldn't swear to that, I haven't tested it, but you have the feeling that you do because you hit it so well once you concentrated hard on watching it.* And if you don't watch it that closely then maybe you may hit it off-center. It makes that much difference.

Q: When you are at the net and your opponent is trying a passing shot, what kinds of things are you thinking about?

A: You have to try and remember how good your opponent is and what his preferences are. He has definite preferences, might be better down the line, he might be better across the court, he might be better across court when he is running, he might be better down the line when he is stationary, that type of thing. You should also note your opponent's body position, where he looks before he hits, and how he swings through the ball. All that comes into play.

Q: Then you can read the lob.

A: Yes. It is very seldom you can't read it. You might read it late, but you still can read it.

Q: How important is it to direct the ball to a specific area of the court?

A: The angle of the ball is most important in keeping control of the game. Quite often you will give the opponent the ball to open up a corner that is more difficult for him to hit in. You may change the angle to let it down the line a little more, because he has to change the direction of the ball. The ball is spinning, it comes to his racquet, he can redirect it. In that way, there is more strategy. The obvious thing is from an angle you go back to an angle but there are exceptions which give you control of the game.

Authors' Note: We do not believe it is possible to see the markings of a tennis ball in flight.

Authors' Note: Many of the professionals who claimed they could see the ball right into the racquet were shocked when shown photographs of them in action — their eyes were not focused on the ball.

One never changes direction of a hard-hit ball. The body is going one way, in one direction, so there is a natural movement whether it is, for instance with some players, just letting go; it might be down the line but it is still the natural flow, and if you force him to redirect to the place where he is not that comfortable then you have a better chance of beating him.

Q: When you were playing, all the balls were white. Now they have converted to the yellow ball. Would you find it difficult now switching back from the yellow ball to the white ball?

A: I don't know. The white is harder to see now. It is a little harder to see when a person dressed in white happens to hit the white ball that crosses his body in some way, or if in the background there happens to be somebody there in a white shirt or shirtsleeves. No matter what the colour of the ball, it doesn't make that much difference from a distance. I guess it makes a difference when it is close to you. The difficulty with the white ball is that if you happen to play on a surface that is not clean, such as asphalt or a surface with red clay, the ball will pick up the colour and be made grayer or redder thus making it harder for you to see.

As the game goes on, the ball becomes harder to see because it picks up more and more of the colour of the court's surface.

Q: Why was yellow chosen as a colour?

A: It's a light colour. They have tested everything. You have seen pink and orange on the courts.

Q: I thought the orange was selected because they wanted to get contrast with the blue background that they use for television. They use a blue court for TV because the green vibrates on the TV screen.

A: Yes, it does. A lot of colouring has to do with the colour of the court. But if the ball is fairly high or if you are receiving a first serve and the background is light as against the sky and there are no clouds, then it is very difficult to see the ball. It doesn't matter whether the ball is yellow or green in that case. But if the background is light then the yellow ball is better than the white.

Q: When you mention the state of the court, like a clay court as opposed to a grass court, maybe it is easier to see the ball on a clay court after the bounce.

A: Well, there is plenty of reason why they have adopted HAR-TRU courts. They are usually grey/green. I don't know, maybe it is for the contrast. But it's possible that the coloured ball came in after the courts started to be colourful also. There was no need for it before. If the courts were all grey or grey/green as they were, the white ball was perfect on them.

Q: Do you find it easier to hit overheads on a cloudy day as opposed to a day where the sky is clear?

A: If you have a sky that doesn't have a cloud you can't judge. I remember the year of the Victoria Davis Cup matches. For about a week it was never cloudy. I was missing my overheads. The day of the matches was very cloudy and it was as though I had been hitting them perfectly all along.*

Q: Do you think it is the contrast or do you pick up depth of the ball through your depth perception?

A: It must be the depth. You can't judge where it is when there is no cloud and no contrast.

Q: What about when you serve?

A: No, that doesn't matter. It is more by habit.

Q: Do you do anything special when you are serving on a bright sunny day?

A: Well, it depends on the time of year. In June, for instance, the sun is a little bit lower and that gets very complicated. You have to vary your serve in some way, which may mean you can lose some of its effectiveness.

Q: How do you vary it?

A: Well, by throwing it to the side or standing at a different spot on the baseline. Throwing it up in the air is the most important part of the serve. And if you have to throw it a little differently you can lose power or rhythm. So the only thing you can tell yourself is that it's the same for both. A left-hander might not have any problem at all. It depends on how the court is situated and where the sun is.

Authors' Note: On a clear day you only have your binocular vision to rely on. The lob shot is particularly difficult to make in these conditions.

Q: Are all the pro courts set in a certain way?

A: Yes, north-south normally. But let's say the sun is on one angle of the court. The right-hander will see it in one position and the left-hander in another. The left-hander might not be bothered by it at all.

Q: When you are running for a wide ball, do you try and stop before you hit it?

A: We always try to get there and be ready in position and await the ball. This isn't always possible in a game but certainly we are in a better position to see the ball when we are in the standing position.

Q: In pro games can some of the players disguise their shots?

A: You have to use wrist movement.

Q: You mean just at the last minute you flick your wrist?

A: You always flick your wrist. When you look in the books, they say don't use wrist but it is impossible to play a decent game. You try and use a little in the regular shots if you want to make a decent backhand — you must flick your wrist.

Q: Can you still follow the ball as it comes off a bounce or do you just anticipate where it is going to bounce?

A: If the person serving is on his second serve and you want to know whether you should make an offensive shot or not, you have to know exactly where the ball is going to bounce. If it is close to the back of the service line, you just return the ball but if it bounces in you will probably go in and make a harder shot. Naturally, there are so many factors that you have to think about and watch that maybe watching the ball is only one of many and you can't put all your concentration on it. But if you did concentrate strictly on watching the ball and didn't worry about any other factor then you could probably see a lot more and a lot later, I mean up to the time of hitting. For some time you might be hitting under the ball and you decide to hit six inches higher and then you start playing well. I don't know if that has anything to do with sight or not but I know at the start of each year when I used to play a fair amount, and in England, particularly when I started to play there, I was hitting the ball very badly and all of a sudden I decided that instead of hitting here I am going to hit five inches higher. I started doing that and my hitting was fine. Whether it was my vision or just my timing, I don't know.

Q: You were hitting the ball at a higher level than where you were anticipating it to rise.

A: Yes, I was always hitting with the top part of the racquet. That could have been my vision, it could have been my lack of judgement.

Q: Had you not played for a while?

A: I hadn't played for months.

Q: And you could actually move your racquet up five inches mechanically to hit above the ball?

A: Yes, instead of hitting up here at the top of the racquet, I would try to hit down low on the racquet and I was hitting very well. After a while you don't even have to think about it. Maybe it was a physical readjustment.

Q: Do you think you can see better on one side than on the other?

A: I think we all have strengths and weaknesses, for different aspects of the game — including visual skills. I'm sure I see better on my left side.

Q: You see better on your left side and you are right-handed?

A: Yes. I can do anything here on the backhand side whereas on the forehand side I miss a lot.

Q: Which is your dominant eye?

A: I would think the right but I am not sure.

Q: It is very easy to test — look at the tv aerial and point. Which finger is on target and which is off target?

A: I am pointing at the TV aerial and the left eye is aligned with the aerial.

Q: The left eye is your dominant eye.

Dibbs mentioned that Connors is terribly hard to beat because his vision is so superb that he can pick up all the visual clues earlier than anyone else.

A: I would think that that is very correct. I saw Connors with Newcombe at that first challenge match. I've never seen anything like it. Newcombe is a fantastic server and Connors was there returning the serve at 100 miles per hour . . . you could hardly see the ball.

Q: I was watching Newcombe practice for that match at Newcombe's ranch in Texas. When he came back after he had lost the match he didn't seem that upset because he lost but he said Jimmy Connors was hitting the returns harder than he, Newcombe, was serving them.

A: That was the best played match I had ever seen in my life.

Q: What are some of the differences in the type of game played today than was played some years ago in your day?

A: Players hit way more spin today than they did years ago. They have the topspin lob nowadays and in 1954 and 1956 there were one or two in the world that had the topspin lob. Seixas was the one and only who hit the ball with a bit of a Western grip. Now everybody has a topspin lob and the second greatest improvement is the two-handed backhand. There is no question. It means two things. One is that players have been playing longer. If they use two hands it is because they started too young to be able to do it with one hand. But it is a shot that is much more precise than any other because you can make it a lot quicker and hit it a little later and still make a very good shot.

Those are the major improvements. Aside from that, the top players are no better; there are many, many more good players in the world and strategies are better. That's why a lot of mediocre players are now good players because of the two-handed backhand.

Q: During some of the pro matches the linesman will call a shot out or in and a player will call it the opposite way and they get into a fight. Who really sees the shot better?

A: I would think the player, because of the angle at which the linesman sees it. As the ball approaches the line, the linesman is focusing on that area and only has so much time to see the ball whereas the players see it all the way through. I feel the player has the advantage there.*

Q: Is it easier to see a ball on the indoor courts or is it easier to see on the outdoor courts?

Authors' Note: The linesman whose head and eyes are stationary is in a better position to judge.

A: Nothing is better than daylight. No light has been perfected yet although some of the mercury types, or indirect lighting, give you a good background, but if you still have those lights that hang over, usually the ball arrives before you are set, making a return impossible. Also, the light has to cover all parts of the surface. That's why indirect lighting is quite good, but if the lights are directed directly down then some shots will be lost in the shadows. There are some players who cannot play in the lights at all no matter how good they are.

Q: That's outdoor evening light as well as indoor light?

A: Yes, and some players will object to playing in any tournament that goes under the lights because they know that it could affect their play.

Q: Do you think the large frame racquets offer any advantage?

A: I think they offer an advantage to an older person who has gotten a little bit slower. Before he used to connect with the ball on the frame. With the bigger racquet he may hit it on the strings.

Q: Is it easier to return a flat hard serve as compared to a spin serve?

A: I would expect that most people would like returning a flat serve. I don't, mainly because I have unorthodox strokes. It takes a spin longer to reach the opponent so there is more time for the receiver to react.

Q: Going back to the volley, do you think you can actually follow the ball all the way to the strings?

A: One angles one's racquet which makes you believe that you just about see the ball because you turn the racquet to meet it. You have to. You have a good feeling about what the racquet is going to do. Quite often you are apt to make a little funny shot but you anticipate the angle and adjust your racquet in order to hit.

Q: You are watching the head of your racquet?

A: Yes, so I would suspect that you are seeing the ball too.*

Q: Do you think the average top player breaks down the

Authors' Note: Not only can you not see a moving ball, the eye cannot see a moving racquet either.

components of the game, or does he do it more or less by instinct and natural reflexes?

A: I think that most players analyze their mistakes and make the necessary corrections. Often the better the player you are the less time that you need to implement the new techniques. I know that twenty years ago it took me weeks to get back into top form if I hadn't been playing for a long period of time. Today it takes me three days to get back to the point where I am hitting well. Call that experience if you wish but I know how to take a backhand apart and there are eight to ten things you have to worry about. If you are not doing one of them very well, then maybe there's one you have to try and work on. A few years back I was just hitting and hitting and finally it came about. But now in five or six practices, I am ready.

5 An Interview with Renee Richards

As we are interested primarily in the visual side of tennis, we felt extremely fortunate to obtain an interview with Renee Richards. She is an ophthalmologist with strong clinical expertise in ophthalmology. She has had enviable academic training attending outstanding institutions such as Yale University. But besides being an expert on eyes and visual function, she has played tennis in the ranks of the professional circuit and has enjoyed world ranking. She has played in most of the top tennis tournaments and has played against the world's greatest players. Her tennis career and her ophthalmic aspirations have moved along side by side as she has matured. It has been an incredible blend of talents, and for us, an opportunity never again to be met.

To add a further dimension to this interview, Dr. Richards also happens to wear contact lenses, so her response as a patient wearing this visual device must be appreciated. She understands the optics of contact lenses and their special application to a fast sport like tennis in which she has such a vital interest.

We must pause to thank Mr. Bernard Gluckstein of Toronto who obtained this special interview for us at the United States Open. Mr. Gluckstein is a tennis enthusiast, a devotee to fitness, and a top tennis photographer.

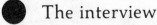 The interview

Question: Jimmy Connors is known to have 20/10 vision. Can you explain what this means and whether such eyesight is an advantage?

Answer: 20/20 vision means that you see at twenty feet what

a normal person sees at twenty feet. 20/10 vision means that you can resolve at twenty feet what a normal person has to bring up to ten feet in order to see. It is better than normal vision. Having this superior vision for a stationary target may not give him any advantage for a moving ball unless he has that kind of visual system that does better with a moving object rather than a stationary object. When his body and eyes are still he may be able to focus on his opponent a little easier than the average person.

Q: At the level of professional tennis, where points are made through the application of speed, is vision secondary to anticipation?

A: Having good vision is important but in a fast-moving sport a player can't wait for the happening, he or she must anticipate it. So anticipation is a major complement to vision. Ordinary stationary vision, the type used in reading where the eye is still and the print is still, is really not relevant to tennis. What is important here is the tracking ability of the eye.

Q: What is meant by the tracking ability of the eye?

A: There are two different kinds of tracking or gaze movements. One is an optically elicited movement which depends on catching sight of the ball in space. This varies directly with the size of the object and is more apparent close in when the ball appears larger. It depends on one's Snellen visual acuity or the resolving power of the eye. The tracking part of tennis depends on the following gaze movements which are under voluntary control and mediated by the frontal lobe of the brain. The optically elicited movements are largely involuntary and controlled by the occipital cortex of the brain. For tracking movements of the eye, a player has to pay attention to the ball. Once a ball is sighted by the optically elicited movement of the ball, then it must be tracked or followed by the frontal lobes. If you're tired, and not concentrating, then you will not track the ball properly.*

Q: Can the eye stay on the ball throughout its course?

A: Ideally you would like to see the ball travelling in its entire

---

Authors' Note: Both optically elicited eye movements and following gaze movements are too slow to follow a ball.

course directly to your racquet. Then you could guarantee that you would hit with the center of the racquet every time. In any shot, there is always a point that you lose the ball. This is enhanced by the movement of the racquet. You certainly could see the ball closer to impact if the racquet were absolutely still. But since a player has to go into a windup, turn the body and shift his weight to prepare for a stroke, there is not much opportunity to see the ball. If you wait for the ball to come close to the racquet, you may see it but you are not going to make much of a shot.

Q: At what distance does a player lose sight of the ball?

A: It varies with the kind of shot being made and the velocity of the ball coming at you. If you're trying to return a Roscoe Tanner serve, you may see the ball coming over the net, but the rest is all done by timing reaction, reflex movement, and memory of where you think the ball is going to be. Some players like Ken Rosewall and Pancho Segura used to watch the ball quite closely and follow it as long as possible — others do not bother to try and follow the ball and play superb tennis. Nobody can see it all the way, but some players do see the ball longer than others.

Q: Do you get a better view of the ball near the bounce?

A: Definitely. On the ground there is a frame of reference. In the air you can't tell whether it is back, forward, or how high it is. Besides, once the ball hits the ground it loses some of its energy and its velocity is reduced. When the ball hits the court you get some idea of where it is and how high it is. The absence of a bounce makes the volley shot so difficult. On the other hand, the bounce makes the groundstroke so much easier.

Q: As you can't see the ball, is much of the stroke dictated by memory?

A: Yes, it is like a juggler who has five balls and he keeps them all in the air. He certainly can't follow five balls at once. The same is true in tennis. There is a certain rhythm to each stroke which is automatic and doesn't really depend on visual control.

Q: Does the orientation of the body to the ball affect the way you see it?

A: If your body is directly in line with the ball you see it better. For example, at the net, if you volley and allow the ball to move to the sides, you won't see it. If you volley in front of you, then you have a better chance of seeing the ball.

Q: Why is night play so difficult?

A: It is particularly hard to hit an overhead smash. There are no clouds or reference points for the ball so you don't know where the ball is. What I do is actually look through my racquet to chart the ball. I am essentially placing a grid over the flight pattern of the ball. Some players track the ball with their free hand. At any rate hitting a lob is difficult — at night it is murder.

Q: Does the colour of the court affect your play?

A: A green court seems to be soft on the eye as there isn't any glare factor and a yellow ball has the best contrast. If the court is a dull finish, it is helpful especially if it offers contrast to the ball. I have played on blue courts and these were terrible because of the glare factor. Tan courts are also taxing for the eye as there isn't sufficient contrast between the court surface and the ball.

The colour of the ball should also be yellow because it can be seen under the widest variety of illumination. Most tournaments routinely use yellow balls except for Wimbledon which still employs white balls. For a fast serve, like Roscoe Tanner's, the use of a white ball is a definite advantage for him, as it makes the return of service even more difficult for his opponent. Incidentally, playing at night also favours the player with a bullet serve and probably was a factor in Tanner's defeat of Bjorn Borg at Forest Hills in 1979.

Q: How do the professionals return a serve like Tanner's which may travel at 130 miles per hour?

A: Well, it certainly doesn't require strength as many women can return the strongest male service. Rosie Casals can return anybody's serve in mixed doubles including the cream of men competitors. Tracey Austin can hit the fast ball back without much difficulty. To hit a cannonball requires anticipation, fast reflexes, and a willingness to move forward into the ball.

Any player loses sight of the ball once it travels over the net. You must anticipate early and watch the ball the moment it is struck.

There is another phenomenon called critical flicker fusion. If you flash lights at somebody in rapid enough sequence the lights will appear as a blur — you won't see the lights discretely. In a slow sequence, the individual lights will be seen. A great return of service player, like Jimmy Connors, may have better critical flicker fusion ability, or the facility to make out sequences of the ball travelling fast, than other players.

Q: Are glasses a disadvantage to a player?

A: From a standard point of visual acuity, there is really no disadvantage. However, a near-sighted person would see the ball clearly but smaller with glasses. Another disadvantage is the distortion by the thicker edge of the spectacles at the periphery. Practical objections to glasses is that they may move, fog up, or become covered with sweat.

Most of the disadvantages are obviated by wearing contact lenses. The only residual problem with contact lenses is excessive glare. I wear soft lenses, and I still am annoyed by the irritating effects of glare. Hard lenses create more glare but soft lenses do not eliminate it. The only other problem I have with soft lenses is that they frequently dry at the end of the day. So before a match, I may take them out and add a little hydration to freshen them up.

Q: Do contact lenses ever pop out during a match?

A: I have never had my soft lenses dislodge or be ejected by my lids during a match. A major advantage of soft lenses is that they make me feel more secure. I have been wearing them on tour for one year and although I am more comfortable with soft contact lenses, I can't really say they have added measurably to my overall tennis performance.

Q: When a player is moving, is his ability to see the ball impaired?

A: To an extent it depends on how you run. Some players actually run with their head facing the ground. For instance, Tracey Austin frequently runs with her head down into the court. Ideally, the best way to run is with your head facing the net with the racquet in ready position.

Q: Does anybody see the ball on a half volley?

A: A half volley is a timing shot in which you don't really see the ball in the area of the bounce. The proper execution of a half volley depends more on experience and feel than visual control.

Q: Do you think a player is in as good a position as a linesman to call the ball in or out?

A: The linesman has a better opportunity to call the ball in or out. He is basically doing one thing — watching the line.

A player is following the ball. He may or may not see the bounce so he or she really doesn't know if the ball is in the court, on the line, or just out.

A linesman is taught to watch the line. He does not watch the motion of the serve or the movement of the ball. Personally, I don't know whether the visual judgement for a linesman is better watching the line or the ball. Whatever method the linesman employs, he certainly has a better chance of calling shots correctly as his head and eyes are not moving. In a dispute, the better judgement really belongs to the linesman.

Q: Is good peripheral vision a factor in a tennis match?

A: Generally, I follow the ball with my central vision and I am very aware of my opponent's moves through my peripheral vision. For instance, if I see my opponent coming up to the net, I am going to change my tactics and perhaps use a passing shot such as an overhead lob or a down-the-line return. The key word is see because you don't really see too well through your peripheral vision. It is not possible to see one's opponent and the ball at the same time. Some people actually take their eye off the ball to look at their opponent but this is not a good visual tactic. A player should have the entire court in his peripheral vision and be aware of the activity in that court without actually looking at the object of regard. It takes concentration and awareness to keep one's eye receptive to the movement in one's peripheral field. Fatigue is perhaps the greatest obstacle to visual awareness. It causes contraction of the visual field and depresses concentration.

6 An Interview with Eddie Dibbs

By the age of twenty-seven, Eddie Dibbs was a three-time winner of the German Open Tournament and one of the rising stars on the professional tennis circuit.

He left the University of Miami in 1973 to turn professional and his earnings in prize money have increased each season, including the 1975 season during which he missed the World Championship Tennis (WCT) tour because of mononucleosis. In 1975, he defeated Jimmy Connors and Arthur Ashe to win the Dewars Cup and he defeated Ashe to reach the quarterfinals of the U.S. Open at Forest Hills. In 1976, he defeated Forest Hills champion Manual Orantes to win the German Open.

A native of Brooklyn, N.Y., the Dibbs family moved to Miami when Eddie was five years old and he began playing tennis at the age of eleven. While in high school, he was a shortstop on the baseball team, but he gave up that sport to concentrate on tennis at the urging of his father.

On the court, the 5' 7", 160-pound Dibbs is noted for his groundstrokes and two-fisted backhand, a style best suited to the clay courts of Europe, although he is currently developing more of a net game.

Off the court, Dibbs likes to relax at the beach at his Miami Beach home and play a little paddleball and basketball.

We were fortunate to have Raymond Stein, a ranked Canadian tennis player who played for the University of Pennsylvania, conduct this interview. We were able to complete a full ophthalmological assessment of Mr. Dibbs just prior to his tournament victory.

Eddie Dibbs hits a two-handed backhand. The key to hitting the ball in a zone of fog is to hit well in front of the body. (The Toronto Star)

● The interview

Question: In many sports the psychological, physiological, and physical factors have considerable bearing on the success of a professional athlete. The visual aspects and visual clues in sports appear to us to be the most significant factors for a topnotch athlete who wishes to achieve success. How dependent are you on good vision in a game?

Answer: Today good vision is crucial to my game and to my success on any day that I am on the court. However, during my college days at the University of Miami, I had glasses but didn't realize how poor my vision was. I played most of my matches without glasses. When I told a good friend of mine, an ophthalmologist, that I had trouble picking up the ball, he suggested I come in for an examination. He couldn't believe it. My vision was so bad —20/400 — he couldn't believe I was hitting the ball.*

Q: How old were you then?

A: I was in college, around age twenty. He fitted me with hard lenses. Actually, without the lenses, I couldn't even see the ball on the other fellow's side. It was just like a little blur coming back over at me. It was joke when I look back on it now.

Q: How long have you been wearing soft contact lenses?

A: As I mentioned, I started off with hard contact lenses. When I played indoors I had a tremendous glare off the lights. With the soft ones, now I have no glare at all. I have been wearing them about seven years and they have made a significant improvement to my game.

Q: Did you find the hard lenses fell out at all during play?

A: Actually, they did pop out a couple of times during play of a match. The biggest problem with hard lenses was sliding them over the eye. I prefer soft lenses.

Q: Have you had any problems with soft contact lenses?

A: No, none at all. With the hard lens, if it was a windy day, I

Authors' Note: 20/400 vision would be considered to be a condition of legal blindness.

would get something under the lenses. With the soft lenses, I'm not troubled by particles. I don't wear them all the time, however; I take them right out after I play. I don't feel them over my eye when I play. It's amazing how much better you see the ball after being fitted with lenses. I see the ball a hundred times better. It's an amazing adjustment when one gets fitted with lenses and sees the ball so much better.

Q: What we are trying to do is focus on what you see when you are preparing for and when you hit a shot. Are you conscious of what you are watching when you play?

A: Most of my shots are instinctive. I hit so many tennis balls that it has become automatic, like talking, I am not quite sure exactly where I am looking at the time. I try to keep my eye on the ball and watch it from the moment it leaves my opponent's racquet but there is a point in time where I undoubtedly lose the ball and go more by anticipation of where the ball is going to be.

Q: Do you really see the ball actually hit the strings?

A: I am not sure whether I see it hit the strings. Perhaps I only think I do. Usually on fast balls I can see the ball up to a point of about five or ten feet in front of me and then I anticipate where that ball is so that my racquet comes forward to meet it. I go through the motions of trying to follow the ball but it is moving too quickly for me to actually see it when it hits my racquet.

Q: One of the things that coaches are always saying is to "keep your eye on the ball." You are now saying that there are moments when you lose track of the ball, particularly as it gets closer to your racquet.

A: I think when we are playing a slow game where the shots are relatively slow, we can probably follow the ball right to the racquet. As you know, the average beginner is playing a slow game. The ball comes in really slow and he can follow it. But once you get to a B and even a C player, the ball is probably coming too fast and one has to rely on anticipation.

Q: Do you see the ball when you volley?

A: Sometimes if I have good position on the court and my racquet is well ahead of me, I can often see the ball hit the strings but if the ball is coming quickly or I am late in preparing for the shot, I will tend to lose sight of the ball and it will become a reflex based on anticipation.

Q: What about the overhead? Do you see the ball hitting the racquet?

A: In this situation, I have to keep my eye directly on the ball and follow it very closely. It is in my direct line of vision and coming relatively slowly so I can usually watch it hit the racquet without turning my head or eyes. It is important that one hits the ball out in front so one can see it rather than let the ball come over one's head and out of one's line of vision.

Q: When you are serving do you see the ball hit the strings?

A: This is similar to the overhead in so far as I am hitting the ball in my line of vision above my head. The serve tends to be easier to see than the overhead because in the serve the ball is tossed up and is hit just as it begins its descent where it is momentarily stationary and consequently easier to see. The ball is not moving at this point so that one can see the racquet hitting the stationary ball in midair. Also, the serve is easier than the overhead because in the overhead the ball can blow around more and therefore is difficult to visually follow.

Q: Do you think you can determine the spins on the balls of your opponent's hits just by watching the ball?

A: Sort of. However, it is very difficult to watch the spin on the ball just by watching the ball itself.

Q: Can you get any visual clues on the spin of the ball by watching your opponent's racquet?

A: Yes. Watching the movement of the opponent's racquet as he hits the ball gives me many clues as to how the ball is coming. The main thing is to watch the swing. If the racquet comes down the back of the ball it's going to be a topspin shot. I think you can tell very much about the spin of the ball by the stroke and watching the ball hit an opponent's racquet. This is most important to me in my game because by watching the ball hit my opponent's racquet I can tell the type of ball that is coming early on so that I can anticipate my position and my return.

Q: When a ball is coming over the net from your opponent's side toward you, can you detect the depth of the ball — whether it is going to bounce short or long?

A: Yes. I find that if the ball is coming high over the net and firmly hit, it is going to land deep in the court. If it is relatively low over the net, it will probably land shallow. In this way, the net is used as a guide for measuring the depth of the ball. I also go a little bit on the sound of the ball hitting the racquet and my anticipation of the spin of the ball.

Q: After the ball hits your court, can you anticipate how high or low it will bounce?

A: That goes with picking up the spin. If my opponent is hitting with underspin, the ball is going to bounce low. If he is hitting with topspin, you know the ball is going to bounce a little higher.

Q: So you really are watching your opponent's racquet? The way he is going through the ball?

A: Yes, correct.

Q: You can basically anticipate how high the ball will bounce so you can come into it.

A: Yes.

Q: One of the things we seem to think is that when you are running your vision tends to fall off and you see much more poorly. When you run to a ball, do you try to stop just before you hit it, or do you hit the ball on the run?

A: It all depends. When I am playing on a clay court, I slide into the ball. I don't think that I come to a complete stop. You have to get there quickly enough and when you have the time to spare you try to anticipate where the ball will be and be there ahead of time so that you are not on the move and the stroke is not rushed.

Q: When you are hitting a shot do you use your peripheral vision so that you can see where your opponent is moving?

A: I have never thought about this. Maybe for a split second or so, I'm not sure. I imagine I can. Maybe it all comes naturally to me. I really never stop to think about it. When I hit the ball maybe I do glance at the opponent.

Q: When you are playing doubles and go for a ball, do you think you see your partner's position on the court?

A: Yes. When I am going for the ball, I have some idea of where he is.

Q: Is this from your peripheral vision?

A: Yes.

Q: Do you tend to run perpendicular to the oncoming ball or do you move forward into the ball?

A: If there is any choice, I try to move into the ball. First of all it takes less effort because I run less than someone running perpendicular to the ball. Also I give my opponent less time to get ready since I make earlier contact with the ball. Many of the novice players make the mistake of letting the ball come to them instead of going forward to meet it.

Q: They say in the pro circuit that many of the top players have the ability to misdirect and disguise their shots so that they appear to be going one way while in effect they are going in the opposite way.

A: Yes, they look one way and hit the ball the other way. There are some clues however that we tend to pick up such as the opponent's shoulder, the way he is standing, the speed of his racquet as it goes back, and his footwork. If it is an open stance groundstroke the ball will likely travel cross-court and I anticipate that. If the groundstroke is hit with a closed stance, the ball can go either way.

Q: Do you notice any difference between different coloured balls when you are playing tennis?

A: Some balls are definitely better than other balls. The yellow balls are easier to pick up because everything is green in the background and yellow stands out better. The switch from the traditional white ball to the presently used yellow ball has made it much easier to follow the flight of the ball.

Q: Do you find it easier to see when you are playing on indoor courts or outdoor courts?

A: Outdoor courts. The indoor courts have a tendency to pick up a little glare from the lights. On outdoor courts, however, there is always the element of sunshine which occurs at certain times of the day and affects your vision. This is most noticeable particularly when you serve. However, one has the ability to change one's serve by adjusting the ball toss so that the sun is not directly in the eyes.

Q: Some people say that it is difficult to play Connors

because his shots are hit with so much pace. Do you think Connor's success is due to the inability of his opponents to adequately follow his shots?

A: This could be but I have played him a number of times and I seem to see his ball. Connors has unbelievable eyesight. That is another reason why he is so tough. He picks up the ball better than anybody in the game. He can see the toss, spin, and everything about the ball.

Q: Is it easier to hit an overhead smash on a cloudy day or when the sky is clear?

A: In playing outdoors, it is easier to hit an overhead when it is cloudy. I would much rather have it cloudy instead of a clear blue sky. I tend to miss overheads, especially on a really bright day because of the brightness of the sun. Maybe the contrast of the ball is better when there are clouds. Maybe it is because the clouds give a certain depth to the ball that makes it easier to see.

Q: Picking up a ball is usually dependent on the contrast with the ball against its background. If it is in the air, such as when you serve or hit an overhead, it might be better to have a ball that is better suited to the colour up above than the colour that is on the horizontal. Do you think that someday courts might be coloured blue to correspond with the sky above and that balls might be selected based on the colour that gives the best contrast to blue?

A: Yes. The more contrast we have with the ball against its background colour is an advantage visually. When there are people sitting in the stands with white shirts or coloured clothes, it is sometimes very difficult to pick up the ball. The background of the people camouflages the ball.

Q: Do I understand that when you are playing professional tennis, the most important aspect of the game is watching what your opponent is doing and not simply following the flight of the ball?

A: You have to see the opponent's ball hit the racquet. I anticipate my return by the way my opponent swings through the ball and watch whether the ball is going to travel with a certain spin and what direction it is taking. That is why a guy like Connors is so tough because he picks up the visual clues earlier than anyone else.

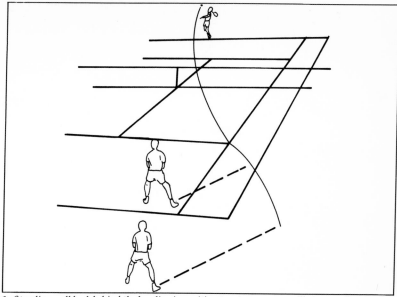

1. *Standing well back behind the baseline in position to return a serve will give one the visual advantage of being able to track the ball for a longer period. The disadvantage is the greater distance that must be covered to reach a well – placed cross – court serve.*

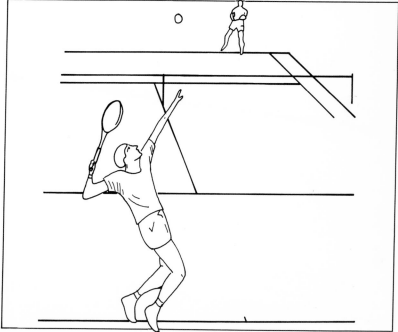

2. *The server watches the ball. His target is based on visual memory.*

3. *Visual clues are important in anticipating the direction of the ball hit by one's opponent. For example, if an opponent's feet are spaced far apart and he is facing the net, the ball will tend to be hit cross–court.*

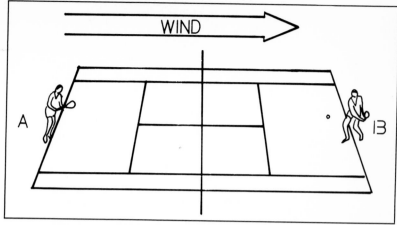

4. *Wind will affect the direction and flight of the ball. In order to use the wind to advantage a number of strategies must be kept in mind.*

PLAYER A
— *groundstrokes should be hit with topspin*
— *serves should be hit with spin*
— *attempt passing shots rather than lobs*

PLAYER B
— *groundstrokes and serves should be hit flatter and harder*
— *attempt lobs rather than passing shots*

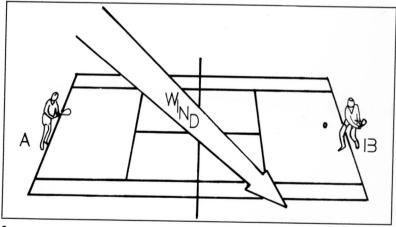

5.
PLAYER A
— *forehands hit down the line should be aimed well within the sideline to prevent the ball from blowing wide*
— *forehands hit cross-court should be hit flatter and harder*
— *backhands hit cross-court should be hit with topspin*

PLAYER B
— *backhands hit down the line should be aimed well within the sideline to prevent the ball from blowing wide*
— *backhands hit cross-court should be hit harder and flatter*

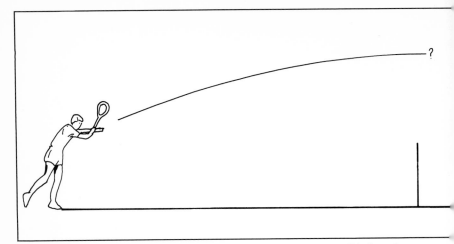

6. *One must carefully observe an opponent's racquet. The nature of his swing will indicate the type of spin on the ball. A ball that clears the net by five feet and is hit with topspin will tend to land within the court and should be played. A ball hit with underspin will probably land long and should not be intercepted. One can identify the topspin stroke because the racquet travels from a low – to – high position; for an underspin shot, the racquet travels from a high – to – low position.*

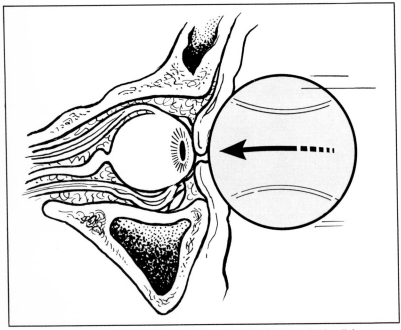

7. *If a tennis ball hits the eye, the eye is partially protected by the bony orbital wall; however, the ball can still cause considerable damage to the interior of the eye.*

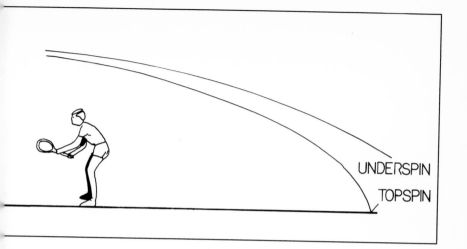

UNDERSPIN

TOPSPIN

8. *Contact with the ball should be made in front of the body to reduce the zone of fog; that is, the distance between the point at which you first lose sight of the ball and the point at which contact is made.*

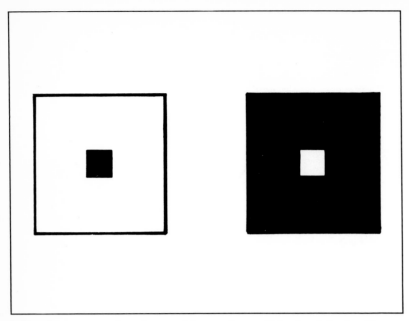

9. *The white space seems larger because white expands space. Going from indoor to outdoor courts creates a sensation of expanded space because of increased illumination.*

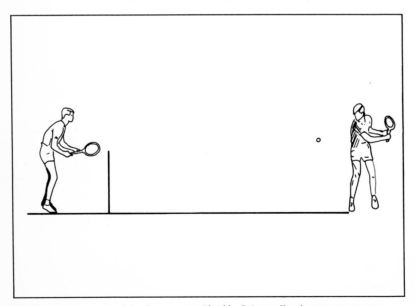

10. *When running, one's vision decreases considerably. It is usually advantageous to stop running prior to making contact with the ball and at the point when one's opponent hits the ball so as to minimize the visual debilitation caused by motion.*

11. *This represents a test for peripheral vision. In the standing position, our peripheral field of vision is 180°. This contracts considerably when one runs so that one has a limited view of an opponent's moves and the rest of the court.*

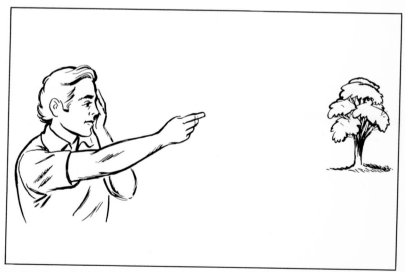

12. *One frequently misses shots played to the side of the non–dominant eye. If the non–dominant eye is the left eye of a right–handed player, he will frequently miss shots hit to his forehand side; if the non–dominant eye is the right eye, he will miss shots on his backhand side. To determine which eye is the dominant eye, look at a distant object such as a tree. Cover each eye separately. With the dominant eye uncovered, the target will be in direct line while with the non–dominant eye there will be a wide gap.*

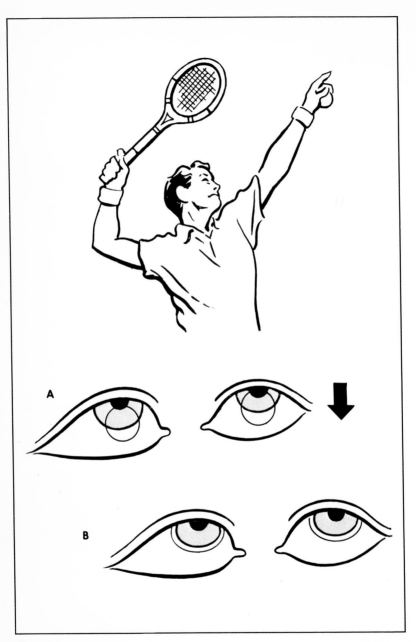

13.
A: *With hard lenses, the lenses drop when the tennis player moves his eyes up to play the ball.*

B: *Soft lenses move with the eye thereby following eye movements in all directions of gaze. Therefore, soft lenses are preferred in tennis.*

14. *Nastase — hitting blind — playing as though he cannot see.*

15. *Visual stability is best when at least one foot is planted firmly on the ground and the body has stopped its motion. Poor form and poor visual control go hand – in – hand.*

16. *Gerulaitis – His eyes look toward the direction the ball came from – not where it is going.*

17. *McEnroe doesn't appear to be interested in impact.*

18. *Solomon — The ball is headed for the sweet spot but he has no visual control over it.*

19. *Ashe is looking through the edge of his glasses to the right while the ball is on the left.*

20. *John Alexander — Despite his hard running the ball has passed his eyes.*

21. *Mayer — An aggressive two-handed backhand executed without any visual control. Mayer is not aware of the position of his eyes.*

22. *Nastase — It is amazing how he plays without looking at the ball yet he is doing it right.*

PART THREE ●●●

Visual Aspects of the Game

7 On the Court

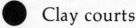

Adjusting to different court surfaces

To perform your best you have to modify your game to suit the particular court surface you are playing on. You must understand the characteristics of each type of surface and you must learn how to change your game accordingly. At one end of the scale, there are clay and synthetic courts that can be extremely slow; at the opposite end, there are cement and grass courts that are very fast.

The game of tennis can be accelerated or decelerated. It is most exciting to play when the fast game is being attempted. However, not everyone can play fast tennis. The older you are, the slower your game — almost as good as a fast game is the illusion of speed. This can be accomplished by playing on a slow court with a big racquet so that the time demands of the shot are not so critical. There is more time to reach the ball, better visual control and, with a mammoth sweet spot in the big racquet, there is little chance that the best part of the racquet will be missed. So the slow player can make it to the ball and make impact with that part of the racquet which will give him the fastest return. The swing will be full and strong and the visual control solid. A slow player can feel like a professional playing on a court with reduced time demands.

Any player who wants to quicken the tempo of the game without adjusting to higher velocity balls should consider making the clay court his home.

Clay courts

Clay courts are considered to be the elite of court surfaces. They give the game an easy cadence and impart a gentleness which is tennis tradition. It is very comfortable on the feet as the player slides easily into each stroke. The sound of the ball is muffled and soft in contrast to the sharp crack of an asphalt return. Also, the court's clay surface will slow the ball down.

Clay-type courts have a top surface that is made of granular crushed stone or brick. In Europe, brick is frequently employed and the courts are often a red colour. In the eastern United States, clay is a common court surface because of the abundance of crushed gravel. The colour is a neutral grey. Clay courts suffer because they need constant attention. The top of the court is soft and loose and requires watering to hold that surface and compacting by a roller to keep it even.

The bounce off a clay court is soft, high, and easy. The court gives a slight edge to the player receiving the shot as opposed to the hitter who finds it difficult to put shots out of the reach of a good retriever. So the rallies tend to be long and demanding but strokes are often relaxed.

Clay courts demand a certain strategy. The net must not be rushed with abandon. The high bounce gives a player sufficient time to reach and see the ball so that the man at the net can be passed either at the side or above with a lob. So clay-court play is basically a baseline game where speed has lost its premium and is replaced by steadiness as a more valued virtue. If volleys are attempted they must be crisp and hard otherwise the balls can be returned. The ace is more difficult on clay because that bouncing ball coming off a hot racquet loses its sizzle once it hits the clay surface. Most players do not rely upon speed with clay and employ spins and accurate placements as better tools to make a serve good.

Cement courts

The pace of the ball off a cement court is very fast. A player who goes from a clay surface to a cement court will find his great slow-motion game shattered by the demands of the fast ball. Everything is accelerated. The ball cannot be seen or followed so it must be hit early; the time to reach a ball is reduced so that the play must be anticipated earlier and the running accelerated and the motion of the stroke either speeded up or very abbreviated. It is much easier to put the ball away so that points are quickly made. The diligent retriever who plods his way to victory after victory on a clay court is invariably a loser on cement which is the preference of the fast and flashier players.

Cement is the hardest of the surfaces and the ball loses little speed on the bounce. The ball bounces well but not as high as a clay-court rebound. Some courts have a cement base and a textured top layer to allow some give to the legs while running and make the game more comfortable on the feet. Actually, the top layers of a cement court can differ so widely that in some cases the ball will skid across the surface and stay fairly low while on others which have a rougher surface the ball will be held longer so that the bounce is a little slower but higher.

The type of game played is predicated on the surface characteristics of the court and the nature of the bounce. Even with the professionals, there are clay-court artists such as Chris Evert whose winning streak on clay is the stuff of legends, and hard surface players such as Roscoe Tanner whose serve and volley game is more suited to a fast court. Occasionally one finds a player like Bjorn Borg who treats all surfaces contemptuously and plays well on all of them. But he plays at the baseline and his great ability is to constantly retrieve even on a fast surface. He uses clay-court strategy on fast courts and comes through this paradox beautifully. He can keep his eyes on the ball longer than those players who are visually aggressive and attack the ball all the time. To accomplish this feat, he moves quickly and must anticipate well to get to the ball and return it with offensive punch.

The fast cement court favours the player with an accurate, blistering serve. A hard, fast serve allows the opponent little reflex time and must be played with a stiffer wrist, a shorter backswing, and greater forward movement into the ball. Visual guides to the location of the ball in space are replaced by anticipation.

The fast ball coming off a cement court travels too quickly for the eye to get a good track on its trajectory, so many professionals such as Arthur Ashe advise merely getting the ball back. It may lead to an easy set-up for a good player but it is better than sudden death. On cement, a spin serve can also be devastating because the ball not only travels too fast for the eye to grasp, it veers to the right or left and bounces quite high. A ball coming off a spin serve can reach as high as shoulder level. These high bouncing balls are the most difficult to return. A player has to put wrist action into the shot and create topspin to return the ball safely across the net.

Cement is the most demanding and punishing court surface. It can get very hot, uncomfortable for the legs, and the fast game will create extra stress on the eyes. Asphalt is a little slower than concrete, but it is still considered a fast surface which favours the aggressive player. It is tough on the out-of-shape club player who has trouble dashing for the net as well as the timid who might lay back for the shots, waiting for the fast ball to slow down at some point behind the baseline.

The fast game played on cement is the most demanding of the eye's capabilities. The following incident demonstrates this point. A world-class player came to us on the morning of a major tournament with a corneal ulcer. He wore contact lenses and his best vision fell in the category of legal blindness. With treatment and the use of ultra-thin lenses that breathe, his vision improved to a more acceptable level although he would still be classified as partially sighted.

We expected him to lose his match; he was comfortable, but he still couldn't see too well. To our surprise, he won the match and the tournament. How did he do it? Simple. He was accustomed to the fast game and never used his vision as a guide to shotmaking. So, bereft of good visual acuity, he was still able to play well.

Cement is really a poor choice for players over forty, for players who do not have perfect vision, and for players who are slow by virtue of lack of fitness or awkwardness in running. Tennis for these people can be enjoyed, but it is best done on clay.

 ## Grass

Grass is still the surface of champions and it is where the roots of tennis lie. As long as Wimbledon remains the world premier tennis tournament, grass remains important for the professional. For the club player, grass is a historical curio, a touch of old England, tea, strawberries and cream, and the pomp of the old Empire.

Grass is fast, but the ball stays low. The surface has give so that the slide to the ball precludes the razor-sharp visual spacing that occurs with cement. By visual spacing, we mean how close you bring your body to the ball before you swing. A player who gets too close has to park his elbow in his navel to hit while a player on the run may not have enough space and gets by by hitting the ball near the edge of the racquet and makes a weak return.

Visually grass is a treat — the colour green is relaxing and easy on the eye. It offers good constrast under a variety of lighting conditions. Unlike a red clay surface, which can add stress to a nervous player's game, grass can relax the anxious player.

On a grass surface the ball may "slide" on the bounce, and the amount of "slide" is inconsistent making judgement difficult. The best grass courts are not absolutely smooth and even, so a "bad" bounce must be anticipated. If you are ready to return a fast ball, and have anticipated correctly, an erratic bounce can wipe out your advantage. The low bounce is difficult for most players on a grass surface because the bounce on other surfaces — be they clay, cement, or synthetics — will be significantly higher. The professionals have to constantly adapt their game and gear up for the most demanding surface of all — the Wimbledon grass. It is a totally different experience as it challenges the player's visual prowess and wits to the limit.

Grass is not too popular in regular tennis play. It is very expensive to instal and maintain in perfect condition. It taxes the tennis player's skills to the utmost. It deserves to be special.

 ## Points on court surfaces

1. It is a good practice to adjust the strings of your racquet to suit the surface. For slow surfaces such as clay, a racquet strung with loose tension should be the order of the day.

This aids control. For fast courts such as cement or grass, a more tightly strung racquet will ensure that the velocity of the return after impact is at maximum. Most professionals string their racquets to sixty to sixty-five pounds per square inch to gain extra power. A good club player will string his racquet to a pressure of fifty-five pounds per square inch. Of course, the more tightly the racquet is strung, the greater the force of the rebound. A very taut racquet is like playing with a board. The ball jumps off the racquet because of the lack of "give." The drawback to a very tightly strung racquet is that the shot is harder to control. For a player like Borg, who has everything a tennis player could want, the racquet is strung to eighty pounds per square inch. Even among professionals, such a racquet is exceptionally stiff.

2. The first time you play on a new surface your biggest problem will be to adjust your timing to suit the height and speed of the bounce of the ball. To aid you in your transition from one court surface to another, remember to always take your racquet back as early as possible; that is, as soon as you can determine whether the ball is coming to your forehand or backhand side. In this way, you will never be rushed in your attempt to stroke the ball.

3. Try and play on a surface that is commensurate with your ability. Clay provides the easiest surface because the strokes are long and the visual control is best. It is the slowest surface and doesn't tax the weekend player. It is a comfort to the knees and a joy for the eyes.

4. Indoor surfaces are usually slow to medium-speed surfaces designed for the needs of the average player. The games are long and the baseline play is rather easy to control with the most points going to the player who can consistently retrieve. Indoor surfaces are the next best thing to clay.

5. The best surface is the one you play on the most. As we have indicated the visual limitations of the game are striking, and judgement and experience are required to estimate the speed of the ball, its bounce characteristics, and the degree of twist-off from spinners. One can easily

visually "adapt" from fast to slow courts, but the other way around is not practical. If your natural habitat is clay, don't try cement — you won't like it, enjoy it, or play well on it.

Club players who play on different surfaces and go from clay to composite courts, to cement, never really acquire any facility in their game because they must constantly adapt to the variability of the speed of the ball. They never learn to adjust their strokes to a given velocity. Their timing is off — part of timing is motor memory, and this may cause a late or an early swing, and part is visual habit which dictates to a player to try and follow the ball into the racquet on a fast court which can't be done.

At any rate, one way to improve one's game is to search out a tamer court surface. If you are losing on concrete you might be a star on clay or on a composite court. If you can't adapt to the conditions of speed, then play the slower game. At least then you can keep your eye on the ball. Your coaches will love you. You will be able to follow the ball with your eyes close to the point of impact. Your strokes will be long and flowing and your game will improve. To put the game in slow motion, the easiest trick is to find a slower tennis surface.

● The indoor versus the outdoor game

Anyone who has played all winter on a tennis court indoors will suddenly find that his game has deteriorated in May or June when he transfers his talents outdoors.

Of course, there is the wind to contend with outdoors. Crosswinds can blow a ball wide of the point played to and a tailwind can make a normal groundstroke sail right out of the court. Allowances must be made for the wind factor but a player already in motion can't readily change his spacing, timing, or stroke mechanics. However, if games are rotated, each player is subject to the same sort of handicap.

The sun is also a "treat" for the outdoor tennis player. The sun causes pupilary constriction which changes the depth of focus. Spatial judgements will be altered because of the alteration in the focus of the eyes. This means that one's judgement of a ball in flight will be slightly different outdoors than indoors. As the pupils of the eyes are contracted, the depth of focus is increased. So the range in which the ball is seen clearly with movement is improved outdoors. Although the visual conditions are better, the eye is not accustomed to the improved lighting so errors are made initially.

The greatest change in shifting from indoors to outdoors is the lack of physical ground clues to provide orientation for the flight of the ball. For instance, the lob shot is much easier to track indoors because there is a ceiling with lights and other visual clues which indicate the position of the ball. Outdoors there may be clear skies and a player has to rely upon his sensation of depth perception: even the presence of clouds outdoors is a relief and a help to the tennis player, as they can provide orientation to the spatial localization of the ball. Once the lid is off the game, as occurs in open tennis, the sense of space is drastically altered. It is expanded, open, and free. The sensory clues to the ball's location, both auditory and visual, are decreased. Reference points at the sides and above are gone; speed is more difficult to judge. Perhaps the only advantage of playing outdoors is that one can hit a lob as high as the one pleases without fear of hitting the ceiling.

Although most players enjoy playing outdoors because of the warmth and the ability to acquire a tennis tan, the quality of the game definitely deteriorates outdoors. It certainly requires more skill to play outdoors than indoors.

The accommodation to light and space is not easy. Light adds feeling of space — white as a colour expands — so that one's judgement of the size of the court is frequently in error. The lack of a solid wall behind the baseline also causes errors of judgement. Typically, the player who moves to an outside court hits his balls long. It takes anywhere from one to two weeks to make the adjustment to the new space while some players never convert completely and require topspin on their strokes to keep the ball in the court.

Some players run into the ball and get too close for a proper swing because they misjudge distance on the outside surface. The visual effect of expansion of space with light can be simply shown. Just look at a white square on a black background and then a black square on a white background, both squares having identical measurements. The white square will give the illusion of being larger.

Some players use weather as a tennis tactic and will purposefully lob the ball to their opponent who is facing into the sun. It sounds like dirty tennis but it is no worse than hitting the ball to one's opponent's weak backhand. It is part of the game. The best antidote to "sun lobs" is sunglasses — some players won't wear them as they feel it shows weakness, but it is the sensible thing to do.

Although outdoor tennis does not have the almost perfect conditions of play of indoor tennis most players like the aesthetics of playing outdoors in good weather. The transfer is not without problems as reference points are gone and spatial vistas expanded by the natural light. The adjustment may require a change in one's anticipation and stroke until the outdoor game feels comfortable.

● Coping with wind, sun, and space

Allowances must be made for the wind factor as its strength and direction will affect the type of strategy employed from the different sides of the court. If the wind is blowing into your back it is good strategy to hit topspin groundstrokes fairly low over the net, to hit spin serves, and to hit passing shots rather than lobs. If you are facing the wind, it is advisable to hit hard, flat groundstrokes and serves and to hit lobs rather than passing shots. If the wind is blowing across the court, care must be taken in order to avoid the wind blowing the ball wide of the sideline.

If the wind blows the ball after the bounce, there is not much you can do. Your body is already in motion and your brain has adjusted for a certain trajectory of the ball at the last second. It is difficult to change body motion or make a change in signals to the brain because the visual signals close-in are not that precise. Fortunately the tennis racquet is large and you probably will still get some of the racquet on the ball, but certainly not the best part.

Most players are aware of the temporary blindness which ensues when looking into the sun for the ball toss. The excessive light creates glare which temporarily reduces visibility. Heavily tinted sunglasses should be used for serving into the sun. The deepest tint, preferably in grey shades, is best. Serving is a visual art and the stroking of the ball occurs when the ball reaches the apex of the toss. At times, the ball is painful to see. This condition results from the sudden pupilary constriction which is intense when looking into the sun. This constriction can cause eye fatigue and affect depth perception. Until the player becomes used to

Borg: He uses topspin to control his shots. He always starts low and ends his swing high. Note: Borg has stopped his motion with one foot on the ground before he hits. His visual control is excellent.

the new parameters of space and the light conditions, he will frequently misjudge the distance of the ball from his racquet and be unable to properly coordinate his stroke.

The problem of spatial orientation can also occur when a player shifts from day to night games. Night tennis also causes an expansion of the court because the illuminated court becomes a white rectangle with a black background. Of course, reference points above and nearby the court are lost in the darkness. Even the professionals do not like night play.

Perhaps the best solution to the vagaries of extended space is to employ topspin. The ball is hit with an early backswing and at contact the racquet comes across to a vertical position and the stroke ends with a high follow-through. A clockwise spin is created on the ball and the air pressure is greater on the top than on the bottom of the ball. This top pressure forces the ball down. Thus the ball can be hit with considerable power and still it will come down like a lead weight.

● Tennis wars — line disputes

Line disputes can send a temperamental player up the wall. To the professional player one bad call can throw off his game and cost the player the set, his earnings, and that precious rank. Ilie Nastase is well known as a player who can blow up over a disputed line call. His tennis tantrums are reputed to be part theatrical but also to that sense of outrage that he has not been treated fairly by the umpires. This became so intense in a recent major Toronto tournament that he was thrown out of the match and forfeited the largest tennis prize to date. John McEnroe also becomes emotional over seemingly unfair line calls and some of the media has already labelled him the "super brat" of tennis. Jimmy Connors is somewhat more contained, but his anger becomes quite visible as he will shake his head with disapproval if a call is not to his liking.

The arguments over line calls is not limited to the professional. It is unspoken controversy in the average tennis club. Why unspoken? Because tennis still clings to its Wimbledon heritage of being essentially a gentleman's game. Hard feelings do occur but they are suppressed — it is not considered polite or good tennis etiquette to vent hostile feelings in a tennis match.

Why do such misunderstandings occur? They arise because everyone believes in the infallibility of their senses, especially their eyes. "I saw it with my own eyes" is a statement that accepts no compromise. One can hedge on a belief or an interpretation but not on a sensory experience. It is like going outside and feeling the rain on your face and someone else telling you it is sunny outside. It is hard to accept. If you see the ball land in or on the line and your opponent calls it out, you can assume one of two things: Either your sensory experience is incorrect or your opponent is a liar. Most people trust their eyes and will fault the opponent as he has something to gain from falsifying the experience. When there is an impartial referee present, as is the case for all professional tournaments, a player will become angry if he feels he is the victim of a wrong line call. If the "poor" calls are numerous, the anger may surface into open hostility. Some players are able to deport themselves more professionally than others.

The crux of the matter is that no one is in a position to take in all the movement of a tennis game. As a player, if the service is fast and it lands in your court, there is a distinct possibility that you will not see the bounce, even miss it entirely. If you are tired and your concentration is off, make that a distinct probability. If you are moving quickly to make a return your vision is compromised by the speed and motion of your body, so there is a better than average chance that you won't clearly see a ball played near the line.

So a player's ability to call the shot depends upon the speed of the ball, the speed at which the player is moving, and visual acuity. There are other variables with regard to eyesight: playing without your distance glasses; contrast — a grey or white ball on a grey court is difficult to see; and illumination, such as the possibility of shadow on a cloudy day.

It is not possible to put one's total faith in one's eyes. Sounds like heresy. If you can't believe your own eyes, whose eyes can you accept?

If you are playing professional tennis, the best eyes belong to the referee. He is sitting in a chair and does not undergo visual fatigue. Nor does he suffer a loss of visual acuity because he is not in motion. He doesn't have to be fast or slow, because he doesn't have to move his eyes to follow the ball. Most of the tennis action occurs in his fixed visual field. It is like watching a game of hockey. The spectator doesn't have to make nimble ocular thrusts to keep up with the action. The motion of the game is seen with little visual effort. Also, the referee does not have any bias to colour his perceptions. Despite his superior visual posture, the referee is not infallible but he should be given the benefit of doubt. He is in a far better position to make a visual judgement.

But most of us do not play with a referee on hand — what happens then? Well, it is customary for the player who is returning the ball to make the call because he is closest to the scene. But is he in the best position to make a judgement? Let us suppose you're playing doubles, the ball is served and it is a blazer. You run quickly for the ball, hit early, and your eyes are on the direction that the ball came from. So you have a situation where you are in motion, the ball is travelling fast, and your eyes are not on the ball — yet by convention, it is your line call. The man at the net who is simply standing there, watching this scene, can do it without flicking his eyes. He is close by and obviously is the best person to make a line call.

Rule #1: The man *not* in motion is in the best position to make a line call. In doubles it can be the opponent at the net or even your own partner. In singles, the matter isn't so easy to resolve. In slow tennis, the player has ample time to see the ball and has excellent visual control.

Rule #2: In slow tennis, the player closest to the ball is in the best position to judge the site of the ball bounce. This is particularly true of baseline shots where an opponent frequently has to look over a net, at a distance of one hundred feet to make an accurate visual judgement. So virtually anything at the baseline belongs in the domain of the player on that side.

Now consider the service when both players are in motion and the action is fast. The server looks up, strikes the ball, and then runs up to the net. He doesn't see the ball after it leaves his racquet because he is running to the net and his vision is poor. When he arrives at his destination the ball invariably has already bounced. The player taking the serve can't keep his eye on the ball too well in the vicinity of the bounce, must move, and generally has little visual control over the ball. Neither player can see the ball. If there is a dispute over the call, the service should be taken over because neither player can really make a sound judgement.

However, should the player who serves not run to the net, he can frequently see the ball better than the player who is receiving the serve. He hits the ball and merely watches its trajectory. He can see the ball well because his body, head, and eyes are still. The opponent closest to the ball has to move to pick up a high velocity missile. His visual abilities are not adequate for the task. The visual advantage belongs to the server even though he may be farthest from the ball.

Rule #3: If both players are in motion and fast tennis is being played, the play should be repeated if there is any ugly controversy. The most courteous players will give the point to their opponent and this method eliminates the bitterness of line disputes. At times a player will claim he has seen the ball bounce, and while the other player will not dispute the call, he will secretly harbour suspicion that the other player is cheating. Usually the point goes to the person who believes his own extravagant visual powers.

Rule #4: If there is any doubt in your mind about the call, give the advantage to your opponent. The win-loss number of points is the same whether you are mutually courteous or mutually hostile. Recognize the limitations of your ability to make accurate visual judgements.

Rule #5: On a slow serve, the best visual judgement belongs to the player returning the ball. On a fast wide-angled serve, the best referee is the stationary server. When in doubt, repeat play or the service receiver should give the advantage to this opponent.

Calling line shots is one of the most controversial subjects in tennis. If it was possible to see the action by both parties, there would be no dispute. The reason that there are differences is that one or both players can make visual errors. To muddle matters a bit, there is the odd cheater in every tennis club who calls balls in or out before the bounce or adds points to his own game by taking advantage of the visual ambiguities. It affects professional play, club play, and can even spoil a harmless game among children. Line disputes adversely affect the game and can be dealt with only if the players recognize the fallibility of their dynamic visual acuity. It is far better than starting tennis wars.

John McEnroe running for the ball. The ball is travelling fast, McEnroe is running all-out. Can a player really accurately assess where the ball hits? We think not.

Recently, an electronic field has been set up at Wimbledon to aid the linesmen to make proper and correct visual calls. The referees are taught not to follow the ball, but rather to look at the lines. This method eliminates the hazard of moving the eyes to keep up with the pace of the ball which is impossible in the fast game. The linesmen watch the lines intently with head and eyes absolutely still yet they may make errors. Why?

There is always the element of fatigue during a prolonged match. The bounce time of the ball is quite short. What will happen to a call should the linesman blink as the ball hits the surface? Blinking can occur fifteen to twenty times per minute so the chances of a blink and a bounce coordinating are quite good. The electronic monitor is perhaps the best way to make accurate calls.

● Glasses, sunglasses, and contacts

● Spectacles in tennis?

Most people wear glasses while playing tennis because glasses will improve their eyesight. Some people who wear glasses for driving or movies, however, will not wear them for tennis because they feel they can manage without them. A slight reduction in vision may be quite acceptable considering the nuisance of wearing glasses.

Why wear glasses? To be a top performer or to play your best tennis it is important to read correctly the movements of your opponent. If your focal point comes out at arm's length or less, you don't see movement too sharply in the distance. Yes, you can improve your vision by squinting but it is like trying to improve your personality by constantly smiling. It is hard to do over a long period of time. So good vision is important not only to keep your eye on your opponent but to assist dynamic visual acuity — seeing the ball in motion while you are in motion.

Are glasses a handicap? Most ophthalmological opinions state that glasses especially in high powers — to correct large refractive errors — make it difficult to play superb tennis. There are so many drawbacks and disadvantages to glasses that, from an academic point of view, they must be considered as a burden in an ordinary tennis game, let alone professional tennis. But, speaking pragmatically, it seems that glasses housed in a set of frames, perched on the nose, do work under the toughest of tennis conditions. Arthur Ashe frequently alternates between contact lenses and glasses and Billy Jean King wears glasses all the time.

In body contact sports, like basketball, football, or hockey, glasses are easily displaced or broken and are seldom worn by top athletes. But in sports without body contact, like baseball or tennis, one frequently sees players of top calibre wearing glasses. The well-known batter Reggie Jackson of the New

Arthur Ashe alternates between glasses and contact lenses.

York Yankees is a case in point. So glasses are not really a handicap for the tennis athlete. The lack of perfect optics is not important in a moving sport because vision is never perfect anyway. So what is missing in resolution and clarity doesn't matter. When you run, your vision can drop from twenty-twenty to twenty-sixty or twenty-seventy. As we mentioned before, running itself is a spoiler of vision and the faster one goes, the worse one's vision becomes. Also, head movement and eye movement does little to enhance vision. The fine points of seeing would be a little blunted in a stationary athlete wearing glasses but it would not make a huge difference in the participation of a fast game where

Billy Jean King prefers glasses while playing.

vision is limited anyway and anticipation makes up the difference.

Once an athlete does convert to contact lenses, rarely will he or she play with glasses again. Sharif Kahn, who is the top hardball squash player in the world, only plays with his contact lenses and feels they are vital to his game. Eddie Dibbs wears Bausch & Lomb soft lenses and he wouldn't be without them. So although glasses are not a prime handicap to the game, many players prefer the relative comfort of contact lenses.

The disadvantage of glasses are plentiful and we shall discuss them because they do have bearing on the game. But bear in mind that the majority of women in the world who play tennis and possess perfect vision could not beat spectacled Billy Jean King and very few tennis athletes could gain even a game or two from Eddie Dibbs regardless of what optical device he wears. While there is a point to be made here we do not wish to go overboard, and denounce glasses as anachronistic (which down deep in our ophthalmological hearts we feel is true).

 The drawbacks

The optics of a pair of glasses leave much to be desired. The eyes cannot roam at will because the glasses do not move with the movement of the eyes. Vision is only true at the optical center of a pair of glasses so when the eyes move off-center, let us say in following a laterally-placed forehand, they encounter the edges of the glass where the vision is distorted. Some people adapt to this confinement by choosing to move their head and not their eyes when they want to glance at something to the sides. If you have learned that the eyes are unable to win a race against the motion of a fast tennis ball, you can assume that a head jerk is much slower. The good players are not terribly inconvenienced by this limitation as they move into a fast ball with eyes straight and do not try and follow the ball into the racquet.

Also, thick glasses limit one's visual field. For wide-angled vision, thick lenses are not the answer. The most accurately focused light rays come in at the center of the lens so these rays at the sides are either distorted by the len's edge or out of focus because of the uncorrected space at the sides of the spectacle frames. But what have you to see at the sides? In singles not very much, because most of the time the eyes are fixed on the antics of the ball. In doubles, you should be aware of your partner. Now if your partner were the size of a bumblebee, you might miss him in your peripheral field. But a person can hardly disappear even in the field of a near-sighted person who doesn't wear glasses.

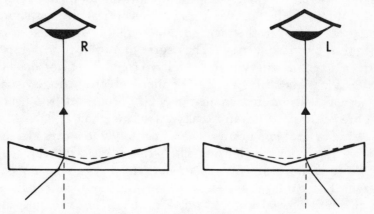

When one does not look through the centre of a lens, there is a prism displacement which causes the image to shift and one obtains false orientations.

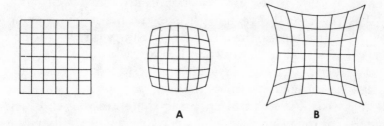

Distortion can be produced by spectacles. A) A strong lens, to correct hyperopia, or farsightedness, distorts to a barrel shape. B) A strong lens to correct shortsightedness distorts a square to a pincushion shape.

While running the head is often bent low so glasses can slip and slide, especially on those people without a large nasal bridge. The constant motion of the glasses causes a power change in the spectacles. It is like moving a magnifying glass up and down. It is annoying, tiring, and causes a loss of resolution. The only reason players are not upset about it is that the act of running is even more ruinous to precise vision, so the added loss is not a major catastrophe. Tennis glasses should have straps to hold the frame, or a flexible nylon temple which can be tightened for play. A rubber bridge is helpful to decrease the impact of the frame against the bridge of the nose.

Glasses are really a telescopic instrument. The near-sighted person actually sees things smaller than they really are. Although the brain adjusts for this optical phenomenon, it cannot adjust to the fact that when images are reduced in size they are harder to see. The degree of minification doesn't affect a tennis ball which is a fairly large object nor does it cause a loss of clarity of one's opponent which is a huge visual object. So although a change in acuity occurs for the near-sighted person, it doesn't really affect his game.

A major problem occurs when a person who wears glasses converts to contact lenses. Then the minification process stops and the brain is presented with images which seem larger. Large images are easier to see but they appear to have a different spatial localization. We judge the proximity of things by size so if the same ball at the same place appears larger, it will be deemed nearer. So if you switch to contact lenses, do not do so before an important match.

The reverse telescoping occurs in the far-sighted person. With contact lenses, the image size of things is reduced and a period of visual acclimitization is required.

The glass-wearing player can be irritated by glare. But there are antiglare coatings that can be applied to any glass lens. Sweat is also a nuisance and there are no windshield wipers for the hot player. There is nothing more bothersome than a large bead of sweat dribbling across one's len's pane or the steaming up of glasses while on the court.

In summary, most of the visual faults of glasses are remedied by the action of the game which limits precise vision anyway. The major objection to glasses is that they are awkward, hot, get spoiled by perspiration, and tend to slide or bounce off the nose.

The major redeeming quality of glasses is that a 3 mm thick lens protects the eyes and acts as a shield. A contact lens covers the eye and is protected by the natural barriers of lids and facial bones but they do not add any measure of safety to the vulnerable organ.

Children in particular should be encouraged to wear glasses which are impact resistant. At an early age, the concept of eye protection should be promoted for all racquet sports.

What should the middle-aged person wear who normally uses bifocals?

If you are going to wear bifocals to play tennis, you might as well wear your business suit as well. Bifocals are for reading and writing, and the focal distance is less than an arm's length for clarity. The range of power may be adequate to allow you to read the label on your racquet before you swing. But that is all!

Single-vision lenses should be worn for tennis as no special device is required to see the ball close in; especially if you are playing slow tennis you can see the ball most of the way to the racquet. The range of a bifocal is too short, the line between the segments is very distracting for play, and the need for a reading lens is nil.

The frame business has now fallen into the hands of the great designers like Yves St. Laurent, Pierre Cardin, and Givenchy. Manufacturers have done such an oustanding job in improving the style of glasses that a couplet, attributed to Dorothy Parker,

Men don't make passes

At women who wear glasses

does not apply anymore. Glasses have been elevated in status and are considered a facial accessory. In their infinite wisdom, the designers have made glasses larger, not smaller — so the new look is larger panes of glass or plastic with large pastel-coloured frames.

They look great but they are awkward and inconvenient on the tennis court. They rarely center and slide down the nose at the slightest provocation. While running, they bounce and come crashing down on the bridge of the nose when they land. The parallax, the induced motion of the environment caused by the movement of big lens, is exaggerated. The edges of the glasses are thicker so that visual distortion at the sides is greater.

So while we admire those chic glasses from Paris, we humbly suggest you return to your old-fashioned frame maker and obtain old-fashioned, but functional, small frames for playing tennis.

 ## Protection from the sun — sunglasses

Perhaps the most universal type of glasses being worn in the game of tennis are sunglasses.

Are they beneficial? From a purely ophthalmic point of view they are neither helpful nor harmful. A healthy eye performs satisfactorily in illuminations as high as 100,000 lux (bright sunlight) or as low as 1 lux (intimate candle-lit restaurants).

The obsession with sunglasses in neither rational nor scientific. Some people wear sunglasses indoors, in night clubs, offices, and so on while others never wear them regardless of whether they are skiing or playing tennis. The shape of sunglasses is determined by style and fashion and rarely by function. Their colour is chosen by what is trendy. Sunglasses are a facial accessory and their appearance on the face is of the sole criterion for their selection.

There are some tips and points about sunglasses that should be kept in mind before puchasing a pair.

Ultraviolet light is absorbed by any glass, plain windows, or sunglasses of any colour so a tennis player need not be concerned with injury of this sort. These rays are only dangerous to the front surface of the eye, the cornea, if they are absorbed without protection from a sunlamp, or at high altitude sunlight.

Infrared light, those rays which cause a sensation of heat and warmth, are not hazardous to the tennis player.

 ## Tinted lenses

Pink tints are extremely popular. They are effective in shielding the eye from ultraviolet but so is ordinary crown glass. They absorb some of the shorter wavelength, the blue-greens, of visible light. The lighter the tint, the less light they absorb.

Pink tints are fun glasses for the tennis player. They are the kind of lenses one wears when colour coordination with one's tennis attire is the most important consideration.

Neutral grey tints are available in variable derivatives and can be so dark that light transmission is only twelve percent. Too dark a tint is unsatisfactory as one's vision becomes impaired. Neutral grey is the best tint as it knocks out ultraviolet and infrared and does not distort other colours in the spectrum.

Green tints are also a good choice, taking out ultraviolet and infrared but they don't reproduce colours as well as grey lenses. Moreover, for extremely bright sunlight, they allow a considerable amount of sunlight to pass through.

Brown and yellow tints

Any tint will work to a certain degree, but these particular tints distort the spectrum and are a poor choice. Yellow tints absorb heavily in the blue region of the spectrum and as such are considered good haze filters. They are primarily used as hunting glasses.

Coated lenses

A variable density colour coating can be applied to any lens. For the tennis player it makes sense to have the upper part of the lens darker than the lower to shield the effect of the strong sunlight from above. The darker upper segment offers better protection when looking up to serve, smash, or to hit a high bounce with lots of topspin.

Colour coating so that your glasses look like a windshield of an automobile can be applied to old spectacles or either plastic or glass.

Polaroid lenses

Polaroid sunglasses make the most sense for playing on a concrete tennis court or sailing. Sunlight reflected from a surface like water or concrete tends to become polarized and reflected parallel to the surface. The "polaroid filter" eliminates much of this annoying surface reflection.

They also make good tennis sunglasses as the polaroid reduces the total amount of light transmitted. If the lens is coated grey, the protective effect from sun and reflected rays is excellent.

They are highly recommended for glare, dazzle, and the other annoyances of excess light.

 ## Photochromic lenses

This is the magic lens developed by Corning Glass Company which goes dark outside when exposed to the sunlight and turns clear indoors. There are two types: (a) The photo sun lenses — the lens of choice for the tennis player — are efficient light protectors and do tint to a deep colour in maximum sunlight and will lighten for cloudy or hazy days. (b) Photo gray lenses also have fast magic and in sunlight the lens darkens to seventy-five percent of its maximum in the first minute. However it is not as efficient protecting against the sun as the photo sun lens.

 ## Children's sunglasses

Most children have great tolerance for high illumination levels. Sunglasses are quite unnecessary as their prime function is to make the eye more comfortable.

If a child wants sunglasses, there is one reason for accommodating that child. If the child is a serious competitor, sunglasses are helpful in keeping the eye on the ball while serving into the sun.

 ## Some misconceptions about sunglasses

1) Polaroids are sunglasses, but many sunglasses have no polaroid filter; they are not necessary in most instances but are the best when playing on a concrete court.
2) Inexpensive sunglasses do not damage the eyes. Expensive ones may be more chic, imported, or even have a better construction but they are not healthier.
3) Sunglasses do not protect the eyes from the sun. They get rid of the annoying symptoms of glare.

4) Magic lenses — Photo gray and Photo sun are not dual-purpose lenses. They are best employed outdoors. They are poor for driving in dim illumination and for prolonged reading. They never get completely transparent indoors.
5) Indoor tennis should not be played with tinted lenses. The reduced contrast creates a loss of dynamic visual acuity, i.e., the ability to see a ball in motion.
6) Sunglasses worn all the time is a poor idea as the eyes become very sensitive to ordinary amounts of light. Then, the sunglasses become a permanent fixture on the face.
7) Most professionals do not wear sunglasses on an outdoor court. The reduced contrast is a worse adversary than the ill effects of glare.

● Contact lenses for tennis?

Contact lenses improve the quality of vision and free the player of many of the hassles of glasses. They are not essential. Billy Jean King has had a splendid tennis career with glasses and no player could aspire for a better achievement. If a player feels that his game is poor solely because of glasses, he needs to be informed. That kind of reasoning is a rationalization, a cop-out, because it has been demonstrated over and over again that glasses in fast sports such as tennis are adequate.

There are many good things to say about glasses — they are the easiest to wear and handle; they are durable and relatively cheap; they are easy to get accustomed to, and with a 3 mm thickness, they are the safest of any optical device designed to correct vision.

Yet, we prefer contact lenses for racquet sports. For every great athlete who wears glasses, there is a comparable number who prefer contact lenses. Our choice of contact lenses as the best optical device for correcting vision is based on the knowledge of visual physiology. It is well known too, accepted, and fully agreed upon by the entire community of professionals in eye care that the overall visual performance of a person wearing contact lenses is superior to that of a person wearing glasses who has a significant refractive error.

A contact lens ensures that the eye is always looking through the center of the lens, regardless of the position of the eye. With players who have thick lenses, their eyes are always running into the thicker and prismatic portions of the lenses when they move their eyes to follow the ball. This causes the image to shift, and one's anticipation of the trajectory of the ball is inaccurate. Some players move their head to keep their eyes on the center of the spectacle and when they do so are invariably late for the shot. So contact lenses offer the best possible vision with eye movement.

With running, the eyes are stabilized to certain extent by organs of the middle ear. But there is nothing in the brain to stabilize glasses. Contact lenses move with the eye and not against the motion of the eye. It just adds up to better vision.

Contact lenses do not become sweaty or foggy and they don't require frames which can get moist and uncomfortable.

Most people are near-sighted and glasses minify the image size. Contact lenses restore the size of things back to normal. Larger images are simply easier to see — contact lenses offer better clarity and more resolution whether the viewer is stationary or moving.

There is a certain degree of distortion from thick glasses. They can break up white light into the spectrum which can create induced astigmatism. All these faults are remedied with contact lenses.

Contact lenses do not slide down the nose or require adjustment. They are small, compact, and offer total freedom from the apparatus of glasses.

● Who should wear contact lenses?

Contact lenses should be considered by any player who has a high refractive error and requires thick lenses and wears glasses full time.

Contact lenses are good practical alternatives to players who do not have a good facial structure to support spectacles. In particular, those people with flat nasal bridges whose glasses invariably slide down the nose are helped by contact lenses.

Contact lenses are a valid way out of frames that do not remain secure during motion. Many people require their frames to wrap around their ears until they are uncomfortable or employ headbands to avoid having their glasses slip while running.

Contact lenses offer another choice to the player who is always distracted by glasses — by the frames, by rivulets of perspiration running down the surface of the lens, and by chafing.

Contact lenses can be worn by anyone who has had clearance from an eye care specialist to insure that there are no eye diseases present which would make them a hazard. Chronic infections of the lids and eyes, ocular allergies, and dry eyes are some of the maladies which would rule out employing contact lenses. People with diabetes or epilepsy have to be carefully selected as to suitability. Also, there are some people who are terrified to put anything into the eyes and can't really handle them.

 ## Children's contact lenses

Contact lenses are not a practical device for children because the power of their lens is constantly changing and they may need annual changes. Exchanging contact lenses annually can be expensive. Also, children may not be mature enough to handle the lenses with proper hygiene and therefore expose their eyes to infection. We have seen teenagers use saliva as a wetting agent for hard contact lenses which is tantamount to spitting in your own eye. Saliva is a very contaminated solution and harbours all sorts of bacteria. Occasionally we have given contact lenses to a youngster — but the child we select is usually very mature and responsible, with a large refractive error, and one who plays tournament tennis.

Tennis players over forty-five are probably better off with their glasses. They will be used to wearing glasses and may not appreciate the new spatial order of things with contact lenses.

 ## Hard or soft lenses — the tennis lens of choice?

There is not doubt that contact lenses do benefit the younger athletes, especially those encumbered by thick glasses. Which to choose for tennis? It does make a difference.

At the bottom line, we prefer the soft lens. There are cases in which a hard lens is preferable, but this would be a minority group.

A hard lens is made of lucite or polymethylmethacrylate. It is a firm, unyielding, and stiff, and requires anywhere from one week to a month for a novice wearer to become accustomed to its presence. It is smaller than the covering transparent coating of the eye, the cornea, and can be dislodged with a vigorous lid movement or a blow to the head or body; it is not therefore recommended for body contact sports. It was so common to see a huge basketball player stop a televised game to look for his little lens on the floor that the National Basketball Association ruled such interruptions were not allowed. In tennis, it is unlikely that the hard lens will snap out, but it does happen, especially on the serve.

The hard lens does make the eye more sensitive to glare. This occurs despite the tinting of most hard lenses. Normal amounts of light may be uncomfortable while wearing hard lenses while excessive light may be almost incapacitating for the tennis player who has to face the sun. The only remedy is very dark sunglasses. This may be a solution when he looks up, but for the rest of the game or when he plays on a side that doesn't face the sun, the heavy tinting may interfere with vision by reducing contrast.

At times the hard lens slips. It is normally very mobile on the eye as the lid carries it up and down the front surface of the eye to allow oxygen exchange. Some players find their lenses hopeless when they look up because the upward and downward movement of the lens is at a maximum with the serve or an overhead shot. The optical position of the lens is displaced from the pupil and poor vision is the result. Some hard lens players have a slightly lighter lens or a wider optical section to their lens, so this annoying loss of fixation does not occur. At any rate, lens displacement with hard lenses is a frustrating fact of tennis life and can be altered by adjustments to the lens.

Should a wearer of hard lenses switch to soft lenses? Definitely not. A hard lens has superior optics to a soft lens. The vision is sharper, more stable, and is not affected by the vagaries of humidity. The people who switch adore the comfort of the soft lens but are never really satisfied with the vision. Also, if a player has any degree of astigmatism, his vision with soft lens will be inferior to that of the hard lens. Recent developments in soft lenses permit the correction of astigmatism with soft lenses. Despite this innovation, hard lens vision is still superior. But there are people who do make the switch and do so without sacrificing vision for comfort, which means little except to prove the exception.

Is a hard lens as safe as glasses or a soft lens? Glasses, if they are truly impact resistant, act as a shield for the face which neither hard nor soft lenses can do.

If a hard lens is hit by a tennis ball, the contact will not shatter the lens but the eye will be superficially abraded. The same surface injury may occur with a soft lens but to a lesser extent. But the most serious damage is invariably from contusion and affects the interior of the eye so that neither lens confers any protection to the eye. The tolerance of an eye to a hard lens is less than that of a soft lens so that the cornea is more apt to be compressed by the firm surface of the lens or by the end of the day starved for oxygen. But there is a new gas-permeable lens which is a hard lens that breathes. It permits the cornea to obtain oxygen through the lens. This type of lens is a mixture of silicone and hard lens material.

A hard lens can be as easily contaminated as a soft lens. One must practice good hygiene to avoid eye infection.

 ## Which lens is preferable for playing comfort?

On a tennis court, the soft lens is definitely the better lens. It is larger and completely covers the coloured portion of the eye and extends beyond it. It is a flexible material and flaccid, so the effect is like wrapping the front surface of the eye with a saran wrap. It protects the eye against wind and dust — an important factor when playing on clay courts. Dust will not bother the eye. The soft lens is large, very adherent to eye, and it will move only slightly —often one millimeter or less. The hard lens on the other hand is small, firm, and moves several millimeters with each blink so dust and debris can easily move under the lens and be trapped by the unyielding plastic. Also, as we mentioned, the hard lens makes the eye more light sensitive. In total, the hard lens stands up poorly against the natural enemies of a tennis player — sun, wind, or dust.

 Can a contact lens be worn just for tennis?

It is the rare person who can wear a hard lens intermittently without breaking it in. So in general, but not without exception, the hard lens can't be worn just for games.

The soft lens, however, can be worn intermittently and doesn't need an adapatation period. It can be worn just before game time and the comfort will be there in about ten minutes. Eddie Dibbs is one individual who wears his soft contacts just for his tennis matches to give him sharp vision.

What is a soft lens? A soft lens is a plastic polymer usually combined with water in percentages of anywhere from forty percent to seventy-five percent. When moist, the soft lens is supple and drapes the eye. When dry, it is wrinkled, shapeless, and brittle and can be easily chipped. They must always be kept moist. If they should inadvertently become dry, like a corn flake, they can be hydrated back to "normal" by simply adding water.

They are extremely comfortable to wear because they drape on the eye and they are at least one-half water. Their edges are thin and soft and they do not strike either the upper or lower lids because of the construction of the lens periphery and the large size of the lens. The lens fits snugly under the upper and lower lids and the thin soft edges adhere easily to the eye.

Are soft lenses the best thing since sliced bread?

No doubt they are the best tennis lens. But

: they are most expensive to buy and maintain.

: they are less durable than hard lenses.

: they spoil easily being covered by protein from the person's tear film. They require daily and weekly cleaning and sometimes only last one or two years.

: vision may be variable depending on the humidity. In places like Arizona they tend to dry out and lose their sharpness. They work better in Florida which is more humid.

: although vision is usually superior to that obtained with strong glasses it is not as good as hard lenses.

When they work well, they are great. Any tennis player who wants to choose a contact lens for playing the game should first consider a soft lens.

Although it can be done, we do not recommend the soft lens solely for protection against wind and dust. There must be an optical reason first. Contact lenses are a substitute for glasses, not a cover for the eye.

● Can soft lenses be worn in the shower or sauna?

Most soft lenses are boiled in order to kill the contaminating bacteria and viruses. If they can stand boiling, they can take heat of a sauna, whirlpool, or shower. They definitely don't melt with heat.

The major adversary in the tennis locker room is the hair dryer. Keep the air flow away from the eyes and the soft lens. It dries the soft lens.

If there happens to be a sun lamp in the locker room be sure to cover the eyes. A contact lens should absorb most of the ultraviolet but, if for any reason, some of the rays hit the cornea, the corneal swelling and pain will be terrible. Ultraviolet injury to the eyes does not become apparent until several hours have elapsed after exposure.

● Can soft lenses be worn while swimming?

Many tennis players belong to clubs and it is natural to go for a swim with one's lenses. It is not a good thing to do.

Most bodies of water are contaminated by bacteria or chemicals used to destroy the bacteria. The eye can be affected by either the bugs or the chlorine. Also, the lenses can be lost — not as easily as hard lenses — but it is not one hundred percent safe. If they do wash off, they are lost forever. Swim goggles are a great idea but we have not encountered a pair that is absolutely water tight nor one that clears the water condensation on the surface.

Do not use drops to get the "red" out of your eyes after a swim. They can discolour your lens. A change in colour may not affect the comfort of safety of the soft lens, but do you really like muddy, grey-brown eyes?

What about "permanent wear" contact lenses? There is no such thing as a "permanent wear" contact lens although there are lenses that can be worn for extended periods of time, up to several months. Most lenses require a monthly or weekly cleaning and need ongoing monitoring by a lens fitter trained to recognize any eye disorders.

Playing tennis without glasses or contact lenses

If your prescription is weak you may be able to play tennis without suffering a loss of visibility. Basically, your vision is poor while you're in motion so the only image that may be a little hazy is that of your opponent. His actions are important for proper anticipation but if you can see him clearly enough, an optical aid may be unnecessary.

So minor refractive errors are best left untreated as the cure — glasses or contact lenses on the courts — may be more troublesome than the disease.

Hitting blind

Vision is a learned experience even though we think it is automatic. A blind person who suddenly is given sight through a surgical operation does not simply see. He cannot recognize that the six-sided square object that he sees is the same as he has learned to identify by touch in the past. Eventually, a blind person who has had sight restored develops a visual touch so that a mere glance at an object brings instant recognition.

Much of what happens on a tennis court springs from visual memory. For instance, the server in his motion to serve throws the ball up in the air and keeps his eyes on the ball. At no time does the server look at the court he is aiming into. In effect, the server's target is a visual one based upon memory of where the court is. In a mindless serve, the ball will either be shot into the net or propelled far too long. Without direction, the server merely flexes a set of muscles to bring the arm down and across. With a strong visual image, the server knows the ball must clear the net so he must throw the ball relatively high and forward, then reach to stroke. The arm must be brought down quickly after impact. Good players study the opponent's court before they hit. They visualize the court, the net, and the kind of motion they need to keep a fast ball in the narrow confines of the shallow anterior court. Eventually, with practice, better players develop a "muscle memory" in the sense that certain muscle groups will respond to a pre-existing visual memory quite automatically. Without any conscious effort, the serve is completed like a rote muscular exercise similar to doing pushups and visual guidance and visual memory is not needed. In its finest form, the player is like a ball machine, with levers, gears, and springs that can spit out balls quite correctly with robot-like precision. Most players never reach that level of motor memory and hence must rely upon visual memory to control and harness their shots.

However, as we mentioned previously, visual memory is a learned experience. So a player about to serve must make a special effort to focus his attention on the net, the dimensions of the service court, and his opponent's position before winding up for the serve. Aiming the serve is done through the racquet. The face of the racquet determines the direction of the ball. The ball is never visually directed or aimed but is sent on its course through the player's mental concept of the tennis court. If the concept is bold and strong, the serve should be accurate. If it is nebulous and loose, the ball is apt to travel too far or too short.

Some people have a strong concept of the court's size and their visual memory is so strong that their shotmaking is automatic. There are players who will hit deep from the back court into their opponent's back court and then argue if their ball is called out. No one who is running has sight so accurate to tell whether a fast moving ball is in or out at a distance of over seventy-eight feet. It is akin to being an umpire in baseball but being behind second base and running while making judgements about the position of a ball that is sailing across home plate. But some tennis players have such a strong concept of the tennis court that they feel they can judge their ball's landing position regardless of how fast the ball is going, how fast they are going, the distance being assessed, and court illumination. It is a matter of having strong visual memory. This is why professionals frequently argue about the landing of a ball, whether it is in or out. They don't see the ball land, but their visual image of the court's perimeter is strong. When they serve, volley, or hit on the run, this visual image enables them to play the game well. At critical times, this strength can turn into obstinancy when it affects their decision about line calls. The player who can find the service court without seeing it and is applauded for it, is greeted by jeers when he calls a ball he doesn't see despite the opposite call from the umpire.

 ## Night tennis

Some factors are not under one's control. If one has to play at night then one has to suffer the glare of overhead lights and the lack of visual clues above. Also, a condition called night myopia might develop, where people who have excellent focusing ability develop a slight case of near-sightedness when attempting to see at night. People who drive a great deal at night get it and complain of not being able to see road signs at night. The same people see a tennis ball late in the courts when playing under night conditions.

Many people who have small errors of refraction and are near-sighted can manage without glasses during the day, when contrast is high and the ball stands out. These people may not be able to function at night and should wear their glasses or contact lenses. Also, there are night glasses to remedy the night myopia and these are effective. These night glasses with a small near-sighted correction can be used by people who normally have good vision and are only distressed at night.

Returning a lob at night is also difficult because there are no visual clues to plot the course of the ball. There are no clouds, ceilings, or other overhead visual reference points. Conservative smashing is recommended — that is, the accent should be on placing the ball to an acute angle at the side of the court rather than a powerhouse smash. The lack of visual aids should make a player uneasy when responding to an overhead lob.

⬤ Points to remember:

1) If you wear weak glasses on occasion for driving, use them for night tennis because your acuity, focusing power, and spatial perception will be altered by night play.
2) Night tennis offers good opportunity to lob.
3) Night tennis favours the player with a strong serve. It extends the zone of fog. The illumination of a night court is rarely satisfactory for the individual player. The lights are either too bright, causing glare, or too dim which reduces dynamic visual acuity.
4) Taking into consideration the drawbacks of night play, the player should play on the conservative side.
5) The illuminated court is really like a white box on a black background. The optical illusion is that the court is bigger than it is. Use topspin liberally on your shots.

⬤ Tennis balls — red, green, or white — which is best?

Yellow-green balls should be the colour of choice for a tennis ball. This colour is midway in the visible spectrum which means it can be seen under good, fair, or even twilight illumination. A red or pink ball is a poor choice as it is not seen well under optimum daylight conditions. White balls merely become grey balls with use. In outdoor tennis white balls lose their contrast effectiveness and rightfully deserve to be abandoned.

⬤ Illumination and contrast

Illumination and contrast are directly related: as illumination improves the contrast becomes greater.

Because of the great speed of many tennis balls, illumination should be optimum to enable visualization of the ball. Many indoor courts and especially tennis bubbles have poor lighting. This favours the player with the bullet serve and places hardship on the player making a return of service shot. There is no remedy to poor lighting which gives extra advantage to the player who primarily uses speed as a weapon in his game. The lack of contrast severely reduces dynamic visual acuity or the ability to follow a moving target.

Poor contrast can result from reduced light while playing at twilight or using dirty balls. The good tennis player should always employ relatively fresh balls as it will make a difference in the way he can respond to blistering serves.

All aspects of the visual game are affected when dynamic acuity is reduced. The player notices that he is late for his shots, his anticipation is impaired, and his ability to call balls in or out is atrocious. In the accelerated game the player simply can't see what he is doing.

Many players unintentionally reduce their dynamic vision without realizing it. They do this by constantly wearing sunglasses. Now sunglasses are used to rid the eyes of excess glare. Playing on a sunny day without sunglasses is uncomfortable and disabling. It is easy to lose the ball when one has to look up when the sun is glaring directly overhead. The sunglasses allow the ball to be seen without the painful constriction of the pupils. Their use is quite valid. However, the same player doesn't think to take off his sunglasses when he or she shifts to the non-sunny side of the court. Without the problems of excessive light, sunglasses merely reduce contrast making the ball more difficult to see. The professionals on tour know this and do not use sunglasses routinely. Actually, they use them quite sparingly because under normal conditions sunglasses simply reduce contrast.

So sunglasses should not be worn on cloudy days or throughout the day into the twilight zone. Sunglasses should never be worn for night play. One can achieve the same effect by turning out every other light on the court. Sunglasses should not be worn when playing in the shade.

Too little light reduces tennis efficiency. Excess light causes pain, loss of depth perception on tracking high lobs, and even loss of vision. Excess light may be uncomfortable and cause the tennis player to squint, but it is not dangerous to the eyes. Good players use sunglasses but do so sparingly. Poor players are addicted to them. Break the habit.

8 Tennis Strategy

● Spacing the ball

One of the important steps in developing good hand-eye coordination is to be able to judge the position of the ball with respect to the outstretched hand and racquet.

Frequently, tennis players have several different running patterns. They run fast for a wide-angled shot and need the speed because they have started their pursuit too late. They can't properly space the extended stroke because their vision on the run is too poor. They reach and hit instead of stopping their motion and then stroking the ball. The better players run slower, and glide or move gracefully because they anticipate. Their approach to the ball is more secure because they are not running at top speed or accelerating.

Another pattern of running involves the charge. Again it is the mark of an inconsistent player. The rapid burst of speed to a slow ball reflects a player's overreaction to a ball he hopes to meet with a solid smash. Normally a slow ball should be a piece of cake. But many players flub it. They rush the ball, come too close to it, and are cramped for the swing. Their elbow is tucked into their ribs and they hit in this awkward fashion. It is a common sight to see a player slam a soft second serve too long or into the net. It is a reflection of poor hand-eye coordination with emphasis on the eye.

To remedy these faults, a player should try and develop a rather uniform running velocity, within limits. He should attempt to move as slowly as possible which is consistent with the demands of the shot. A ball hit with both feet in the air is rarely a strong or accurate hit because vision is too poor for spatial localization of the ball and the player has not planted a foot to hinge the swing.

Teltscher: Even the professionals misjudge the ball. He is cramped for space and his stroke is awkward.

The volley shot in particular can be efficiently dispatched with the proper attack. The ball is moving fast because of the absence of a bounce. It is a poor idea for a player to approach a volley shot on the dead run. Volley shots should be hit while both feet are stationary or at least with one foot very stable. Certainly the body should glide into a volley position and not rush.

On the return of serve many players do poorly. They do not hit the fast balls because they are too slow in reaching the ball for a proper shot — they don't anticipate and as a result move too late or are very slow in motion for one reason or another. They also have trouble with the slower second serve because they don't adjust their running patterns. They may overshoot their hitting position and not allow themselves sufficient room to hit.

We cannot emphasize enough the need to move early and be on time for the next shot. Avoid a mad dash for the ball. You will frequently find you are too close to the ball to make a full, graceful swing. Glide rather than run as McEnroe so ably does, especially to lobs and second serves.

 ## The safest place to hit is right down the middle of the court

The advantage of hitting the ball across the middle of the net is simply that the net is approximately five and one-half inches lower in the middle than at the sides. A low skimming ball which clears the net in the middle will hit the edge of the net on the sides. The safest shot, then, is one that is played down the middle. In percentage tennis, the player will invariably go with the shot that is apt to be safest. The middle is the area of security which gives six inches to the player who has made a bad shot. Not only is there an advantage to the lower net, but the court on a diagonal is eighty-two and one-half feet as compared to a vertical length of a singles court which is seventy-eight feet. The extra length means that one can hit the ball with greater power on a cross-court shot as opposed to a down-the-line shot without going out of bounds. The temptation to reply to any cross-court shot by a ball hit straight down the line is great; however, this shot is one of the most difficult to make in tennis as it requires greater clearance to pass the net and more control to bring the ball into the boundaries of the court.

The major problem in adapting to this dip in the middle of the net is the error of our visual memory and perspective. The net looks straight when viewed straight on. It is only at the periphery of the net the lack of linearity is appreciated. So our shotmaking is done as if the net were straight. Our perceptions indicate that this is so and it is reinforced by our visual memory which gives us a mental image of a rectangular net.

Any player going for a down-the-line shot must raise the ball and shorten the arc of its flight. It is a recipe for a topspin shot or, in a pinch, an offensive lob. Do not use your strokes for the middle at the sides. They just don't fit. They will be either too low or too long.

 ## Head for the net

Good players will invariably move up to the net at every opportunity because the ball can be directed more accurately to the sides or powered straight ahead from the advantage point of the net. Volleys and overhead smashes are the favourite kill shots for impatient tennis players. However, scampering to the net is not a simple matter. En route to the net with a fast run, vision greatly degenerates. When tested, the visual acuity of players during a short sprint is at the level of blindness.

This doesn't mean that one is totally blind (that is, without light perception), but rather the ability to see centrally is functionally impaired. The great Pancho Gonzalez advocates moving halfway to the net and stopping for a moment so that one's opponent can be seen. Otherwise, if the player rushes to the net, he may find that when he emerges from that tunnel of relative darkness that the play is going out in another direction. Therefore it is important to be able to get to the net with sufficient time to stabilize one's head, eyes, and body to have an opportunity to view the next shot.

To play an offensive game you must come to net. To get there, there are essentially four types of approach shots:

1) a forcing serve
2) a forcing return of serve
3) an offensive lob
4) a forcing shot made from any shallow return.

On your way to the net, you may have to stop your run before your opponent hits his shot in order to fixate on the ball. If this is not done, your opponent can aim and pass you with a variety of shots while you are moving.

It is vital to get to the net in time. Of course, you need the legs. If your knees are wrapped in elastoplast, you belong at the baseline. Assuming you can run the twenty-yard dash in good time, the strategy must be to constantly challenge the ball, to go out and meet it instead of letting the ball come to you. A player that backs off each shot in order to let the ball slow down can never really find the opportunities to move into the net. Although playing deep feels comfortable and safe and from a visual point of view quite secure, as the eye can follow a ball about to die, from a strategic point of view the player is usually left in the pastures of the tennis court. He is outside the ring of hot action because he is always backing away from the net. The aggressive player never does this; he moves into the ball early and is always pushing to the net.

Brian Gottfried moves into the ball, racquet out in front to make contact.

The timing of the run is essential. It is more difficult to time a run from the baseline than from midcourt. The risk, of course, is that the ball could be returned to your feet while you are in motion. There must be enough time to complete the run. This can be done by only running from midcourt where the distance is shorter or doing it under the time umbrella of an offensive lob or deeply placed baseline shot. The classical opportunity to run is after the motion of the serve where the momentum of the serve leads the player into his run. In this situation the player moves up to take advantage of a weak return of a serve.

The faster one runs to the net the more one's vision deteriorates. Many professionals advocate gliding to the net instead of running. It is a good principle to observe, because at least with a slower movement of the body and the slower acceleration, one can still keep track of the opponent and properly assess his moves. To arrive at the net without vision and anticipation is simply not a realistic way to play the game. The slower fluid motion towards the net demands more time, so the need for seizing the best opportunity is vital. To create opportunities by becoming a tennis sprinter will win races but not tennis points.

 ## The doubles serve

In singles it is quite common for the first serve to be a blast and the second to be a bluff. In doubles, a moon-ball second serve can be an invitation to an execution as far as the net man is concerned. If the ball lands in midcourt and one's opponent takes full advantage of the gift, the ball could come back faster than the net man can blink.

Normally the server in doubles attempts placement over power with the ideal target being the backhand which is often returned higher than the forehand. A high return is always a good objective as it makes the net game a pleasure.

The server should attempt to head for the net and cover his side of the court. Again, it should not be a mad dash but rather a glide or a few fast steps with a pause to see the direction of the return. It is the service receiver's strategy to hit the ball at the server's feet. If the server is in motion he can't anticipate the ball. But if he pauses, he still can pick up a low volley or a half volley shot and keep the play alive. On a half volley he cannot see the bounce or the ball in close but it is no matter as the trajectory of the ball's movement can easily be computed once the general direction is known.

Some doubles players often play one man up to the net and one man back. Academically, it is poor tennis and you will never be received by the Queen for your play at Wimbledon if you pursue this strategy. But it is the most popular form of club play as most duos are not dynamic enough to move up together, volley, slam, and run back in formation for those lobs. It is not a handicap provided your partner also plays this way.

Doubles — the eye game

Doubles can be the fastest game of tennis because the battle is largely won at the net where the ball has maximum velocity.

The net man is frequently like the goalie in hockey. He may not see the ball directly coming in from the sides but he can respond to it with surprisingly uncanny accuracy. The ball is simply too fast to follow into the racquet and good net players require concentration, readiness, and anticipation to complete a net shot. The racquet must be up and motions of the opponent hitting the ball watched carefully to determine the flight pattern of the ball. Sometimes a player who is moving will not see the opponent clearly and hit the ball well, then scratch his own head and wonder how he did it.

It is possible to project accurately to a peripheral point in space despite not seeing that point. If you look at a book you will not be able to read what is on the pages of a book beside the one you are reading. Your peripheral vision is too poor. However, if you look at a book and someone flashes two fingers to the side, you will know in which quadrant of your field of vision the fingers were flashed and how many fingers were exposed. You can do this accurately without seeing those fingers clearly. The same is true with a tennis ball coming in from the sides. You can respond to the ball's presence; know where it is without actually seeing it clearly. If you are tired, your peripheral vision may be constricted so you may not be able to perceive this break in your field till late. Doubles requires the same kind of aerobic fitness as singles, not so much to keep your muscular motor going, but to keep the sensory side sharp.

The net man should not crowd the net. It is true that the closer one is to the net, the easier it is to deflect the ball with your racquet over the net. But a player makes himself vulnerable to the lob. It is quite common for a serve to be returned, intercepted by the net man with the server moving up so that two people are at the net. One of the best antidotes to two men at the net is a lob that is high and deep or a flatter arced offensive lob. In either case, the person close to the net becomes prey to this type of attack. It is difficult to respond to a lob when one is still — it is very difficult to do it when one is in motion — it requires the services of an expert to do it in fast motion. Occasionally one sees a player not only reach for the overhand smash but actually jump for it. As we have said, the lob is a very tricky shot for the eyes to judge. The only security in the shot is that the ball is moving slowly and a player can keep his eye on the ball. If you jump for the smash, you remove the only visual hold you have on the ball. You are hitting relatively blind a ball that you can't judge in space or correctly anticipate. So don't jump, don't run fast. Position yourself so that you don't have to do either.

Some of the best doubles teams move like a chorus line — the partners moving in tandem, ten to twelve feet apart, dancing up and down the court together. They move together to provide blanket coverage of the court which amounts to a territory of only eighteen feet, the full doubles court width being thirty-six feet. A player can step three feet and swing almost three feet (the racquet is twenty-seven inches long) so that with one step in either direction two players can cover over two-thirds of the width of the doubles court.

Although it is sound to move with your partner, it is not a good idea to look at him. Keep your eye on the action and be aware of your partner's position through your peripheral vision. You won't see him clearly enough to see the part in his hair, but you should definitely know his position without flicking an eye.

The racquet head should be up and ready for the net response. There may not be sufficient time to prepare for the fast shot once it is in motion. Besides, the classical net strategy is to force your opponent to hit up so that you can have the opportunity of hitting down. On very fast shots, you may be using your racquet as a portable wall, merely deflecting the ball and employing the ball's own power for the return. So keep the wall up — it also makes good sense for facial safety. Accidents do occur in tennis and most eye injuries occur at the net.

As with any high speed racquet game, the catchword is attack and the strategy is to hit the ball aggressively. You have a good idea at the net where the ball is coming from, so you move toward that direction. However, you have a poor idea where the ball is going because at close range, the ball can outspeed the eyes. So hit in front of the body for best visual control and also to insure that the ball really goes over the net. Once the ball drops below the level of the net, you are going to have to hit up to clear the net which is a "no no" for doubles net play. It is difficult for the best players and impossible for a vast majority of club players to hit an offensive volley if the ball is below the level of the net.

● Tennis and acceleration

We know running definitely spoils vision largely through the motion of the body. Also, it can be added, the faster a person runs the worse his vision will be.

However, when we relate this information to tennis, it becomes apparent that the better players have to play the slowest game compatible with reaching the ball so that one or both feet are stable when the ball is being hit. The idea is not to run as fast as possible between shots but to glide and move smoothly so there is little acceleration in the body.

If one watches the better players they seem to go from shot to shot in a fluid movement at constant speeds. But watch amateur B or C players. Their running patterns are erratic and they do not move early or consistently. They often move slowly and find that they have not sufficient time to make the shot. So they speed up or accelerate. What happens? Just at the crucial time when they are approaching the ball, they speed up and spoil their sight. Their moving game is poor because they do not know how to move and keep the ball in view.

They think they are keeping their eye on the ball and in a way they are. The trouble is that eyesight is less acute when body is subjected to speed and acceleration.

Virginia Wade has her forefoot solidly planted to ensure a strong stroke.

9 The Tennis Eye

● Problems with depth perception

Approximately ten percent of the population has no depth perception either due to a lazy eye, a crossed eye, a seeing disorder in one eye, or a rather poorly developed depth appreciation from birth. These players can shine when the ball is coming toward them after a bounce, but have difficulty with either the volley or the lob.

John MacKay is a case in point. John was the kind of player who won half his games in the locker room before the start of play. He was six-foot four-inches tall, with rippling muscles which seemed to undulate with each motion of his body. His size, his physical appearance, his coordinated musculature was sufficient to intimidate many players. He was the kind of player who did pushups, situps, and stretching exercises before he played tennis. He was a hard ball hitter who could slam a serve seemingly at the speed of sound. When he hit the ball, it seemed to flash almost instantly across the court. As a tennis player, he was tough, aggressive, and put his taut energies into every point. Big John was feared on the courts by everyone except his wife, who could wipe the courts with him.

His wife Sandy was five-foot-four, a little overweight, had never excelled in sports and against other tennis players was mediocre. Sandy's secret was her lob shots. It was the only shot she owned. Every ball came out like a pizza being whirled into the sky. Her lobs were high, soft, and slow. She had perfected the shot so that they always drifted around midcourt and dropped between the baseline and the service line.

Vitas Gerulaitis reaches back off-balance to return a lob. Even the best professionals have difficulty aligning the body under the ball.

Now John would look up at one of these floating tennis balls, reach with his mighty arm and slam the ball into the net. He did this regularly — although sometimes he tried to change the timing of his slam and would then hit it long. He had two conventional replies to the lob — the short slam and the long slam.

Now there isn't a more ridiculous looking animal than a long rangy tennis player who has just parked a slow moving ball travelling at the speed of a balloon into the net. Every time Big John would do it, his face flushed with embarrassment. He pulled at his hair and would challenge his wife to really hit it.

By the third game, he was talking to himself and swatting his racquet in the air. Of course, the more he blustered the worse he got. He met inner rage with outer rage and he slammed the ball harder. Fortunately for the safety of his wife they all went into the protection of the net.

Eventually other players took note of Big John's weakness. Whenever they wanted a point or take him out of his steady groundstroke game, they lofted a tennis ball to the skies.

Big John would charge at these high bloopers with the fury of a snorting bull. He would run, reach and pow — the ball would go off the edge of his racquet erratically and travel long or short.

Now Big John had a lazy eye and no depth perception. When that little ball dropped from the sky, he had a poor notion of where it was and where it was going to land. He had trouble aligning his body for the correct position of the falling lob, so he had to either reach back and hit the ball long or lurch forward and hit it too hard and low.

Big John was no longer terrorizing anyone in the club when it became known that he couldn't hit a lob with a waste basket never mind a tennis racquet. He tried to return lobs with lobs with some degree of success. Against his wife, he always was given a lob in return for each of his lobs. Eventually he became impatient and would swat the ball. Besides, he hated the lob. It bothered his strong male self-image. Better to be a losing warrior than to win without glory. Against other players he frequently got the ball back with a smashing return toward his naval so he abandoned the lob for lob tactic.

Then he allowed the ball to bounce so that the terrible height would be virtually eliminated. But the ball bounced too high for a traditional forehand or backhand and had to be hit overhead. From the baseline, where the ball frequently landed, it was difficult to smash into his opponent's court. On serves, with a controlled ball toss, his accuracy was a fair fifty percent. *But he had two chances. On backcourt high bounce lobs, without a controlled ball toss, his accuracy was was a miserable twenty-five percent.* His risk-reward rate wasn't good enough to pursue the high bounce as reasonable solution to this problem.

One day, while his wife Sandy was lobbing her way to total domination of Big John, he raised his non-racquet bearing hand and traced the arc of the ball. He found to his surprise, that he could position himself just behind the place where the ball was dropping. Once his body was oriented to the fall of the ball, he started smashing with gusto and confidence. His return rate of successful slams was fifty percent, enough to regain control as the tennis man of the house. But Big John never really dominated Sandy, he just scraped by. He had learned only half of the lesson of the counterattack to the lob.

He didn't appreciate the change of anticipation from a falling ball. On the ground, he was accustomed to a ball losing speed as it approached. In the air, a ball lobbed gains speed as it drops. So if a player waits for a vertical swing, he will hit the ball too low. John tried to overcompensate; he swung too fast and, most of the time, he made contact with the upper end of the racquet face or the frame. He treated a vertically dropped slow ball the same way he treated a horizontal slow ball. He rushed both and hit aggressively.

Finally, he learned to control his desire to pulverize the lob ball. He simply counted until the ball was three feet above his head and then he stroked. He learned this lesson well and Big John grew a little more confident. Moral of the story — the return of a lob is one of the most difficult in tennis. You must learn:

1) How to place your body under the ball.
2) How to coordinate your racquet with a ball that accelerates as it comes toward you.

3) How to avoid glare when looking up at lights or sun.
4) How to compensate for change of focus which occurs when the pupil is small. The pinhole effect on the eye increases the depth of focus.

Big John learned to cope with 1 and 2. All he needed was a pair of polarized sunglasses to cope with glare and the intense pupillary construction and he would have solved 3 and 4.

● The aging eye in tennis

Tennis is a sport that one can participate in until the mid-sixties. Certainly anyone who has played in tennis clubs has been witness to an old tennis player bandaged up with his arms and legs in elastoplast supports to cover weak knees and weak arms, trounce a man half his age. The aging veteran wins because of his excellent anticipation despite the fact that some of the power is gone and lack of agility causes him to reach rather than run.

Although the eye suffers some degenerative changes, which herald the traditional onset of middle age, these changes don't interfere with one's visual perception or appreciation of a tennis ball. What happens is that one's focusing *at near* becomes impaired. The normal lens of the eye, which is like the lens of a camera, becomes harder, less malleable, and less subject to changing its shape as we begin to focus from a far point to a near point. While this causes some frustration at near, usually first noticed through an inability to read a telephone book, it doesn't affect distance vision. Anything beyond a yard is still seen clearly by the normal middle-aged eye. The lack of clarity which so frustrates and annoys the middle-aged person trying to read without glasses doesn't spill over to appreciation of a tennis ball. A fast moving ball isn't seen too clearly anyway at near so its further obscuration by a lack of focusing doesn't really alter the nature of things. Besides, the good players, playing with a high velocity ball, never attempt to focus on the ball all the way in. The average or intermediate players rarely have a problem as the ball is a fair size and the distance of the eye from the ball is usually three feet, well within the normal focal range of the weakly accomodative eye. Therefore, it would be of no value whatsoever and it would be quite a deterrent for a middle-aged person to wear bifocals while playing tennis.

The lack of agility that is frequently found in our regular muscles to move our body does not involve the eyes. Although we may run with less speed, or have less endurance and strength, these same features do not seem to affect ocular movement. The eye can still carry on its normal excursions as well at the age of fifty as it could at the age of thirty. So most visual functions, unless a malady like a cataract prevails, do not slow up the visual appreciation of a tennis ball with advancing age. Reaction time may be impaired and one might be a little late for a shot, or unable to move forward into an advancing fast ball as quickly as one might normally have done, but this isn't related to one's inability to see that ball. Perhaps this is one of the frustrating aspects of getting a little older while playing a sport such as tennis. The eyes can see the ball, the head can make the proper commands to the arms and legs, but the sharp, fast, compliance to these orders is not carried out.

Most older players try to accommodate to their slower movements by allowing the ball to decelerate. By slowing the game down they lose some position and actually have to run a bit more than they would before but there is greater time to hit the ball and the easy visual control is matched by the slower reaction time. However, the slower game is more of a running game as the player must chase the ball. For older players, their best advantage would be to play the fast game, hit early and use the volley and half volley shot, rather than huff and puff around the court.

Although middle-aged people need glasses for near sight, i.e. reading, their distance vision usually remains the same. The only area of importance in a tennis match is that visual acuity needed to see from five feet to one hundred feet — or distance vision. That vision is not imperiled with age. Even if a man is sixty-five or seventy, and he has small cataracts, his visual game would not be affected. Why not? Because the best young athletes do not normally have twenty-twenty vision while playing because running spoils the sight anyway. Any running game spoils ones best acuity, so a little drop in the function of the eye is not relevant to playing the game properly.

There is no cause to even lay down one's racquet because of degenerative vision with age. The only accommodation to age is that some people may require distance glasses to see when they were not necessary when they were younger. Eye movements *per se* remain full and unrestricted throughout a lifetime. Your legs will go far sooner than your eyes.

● Monocular versus binocular vision

Monocular vision simply means seeing with one eye. Binocular vision means the coordinated use of the two eyes to produce a single mental impression.

A monocular person does not possess the visual reinforcement as does a person with binocular vision. If the ball comes in from the lazy side it may not be picked up early. Volley at the net is also difficult because the player is dealing with high balls coming in at great speeds.

So a player with one good eye and one lazy eye should:
1) favour indoor versus outdoor play.
2) avoid playing at night.
3) when playing outdoors, eliminate shots that require depth and visual dexterity. Care should be taken with the lob. Running up to the net after the serve may be difficult and dangerous. It is a prime source of eye injury in tennis. Running volley shots should be avoided by a player with only one good eye.
4) avoid making line calls on his side of the court even if he is sure. He may be wrong even though he thinks he is right.
5) favour his best eye. There is nothing wrong with running "around" a ball if he does it to ensure better vision.
6) play at the baseline where the balls are lower and slower.

Stereopsis is an added refinement of binocular vision. It is the use of the two eyes seeing together to produce the sensation of depth. It is an ability that most people have. There are very few activities that require exquisite depth perception. Flying a small aircraft and trying to land the plane with an automatic guidance system requires excellent depth perception. This is the reason that the visual requirements for commercial pilots are so stringent. In a tennis court, the high lob is the only shot that requires a good depth perception mechanism.

Stereopsis cannot be learned or developed. It is a gift that occurs when two eyes with normal vision and full fields are yoked together in the act of seeing.

● The tired eye

What happens to your visual hold on a tennis ball when you're tired? Do the eyes get tired? Can a sensory organ become fatigued? For instance, do your ears get weary after listening to an excess of music? Can your nose get tired after being in the kitchen taking in an abundance of cooking odours all day? Of course not. Yet your senses can become less efficient after prolonged and strenuous exertion.

It seems natural to consider fatigue in terms of loss of muscular responsiveness and power. You don't start as quickly for the ball, run as swiftly, or have sufficient strength to stroke and control the ball. Every middle-aged or even younger player who doesn't exercise regularly has experienced these muscular wipe-outs.

But tired eyes — it sounds like an ad for an eye wash! You can do calisthenics, aerobics, play sports like swimming, squash, or tennis to improve your body fitness, but what can you do with weary eyeballs?

Ocular fatigue or eyestrain is quite real but is a grab bag term that really encompasses a variety of conditions. Eyestrain will cause the player to see the ball late. Typically the player will say he didn't see the ball until it was upon him.

It is the same phenomenon that drivers frequently encounter under extreme fatigue. They are more apt to get into accidents when tired because they will often state, "I didn't see the car until the last minute." Fatigue causes a loss of dynamic visual acuity —seeing while on the move. Static or stationary vision isn't affected by fatigue in the same way.

Frequently a player who suffers an erosion in his dynamic visual acuity will not be aware of the cause of his troubles and blame it on a loss of concentration. He will say, "I just couldn't set my mind on my game" or "I seemed to lose interest after the first set or I got tuned out somewhere in the middle of the set."

The fast game of tennis requires exquisite timing and if the visual or motor machines are not working, the game deteriorates badly. If a service is coming at one hundred and twenty miles per hour, which is approximately 166 feet per second, it doesn't take much relaxation or loss of concentration to miss the ball or be late for the shot.

What actually happens when the eyes become fatigued? There is a loss of light threshold. What this means is that more light is required to yield the same sensory response. We

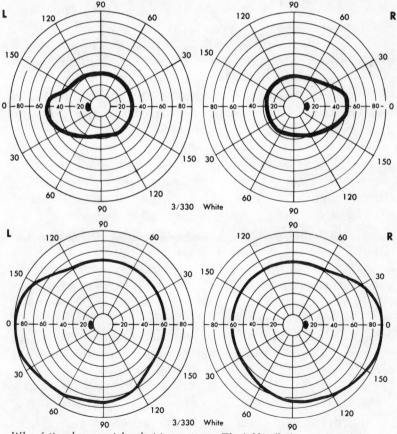

When fatigued, our peripheral vision contracts. The field will also contract while we are running.

did studies on tennis players before and after hard matches. These are the results.

We found that regular vision or central acuity was not affected. In other words if a player could see 20/20 before the match, he could see the same after his workout.

We did field tests. We charted the peripheral field by bringing a moving object from an area of no vision at the side, which is the extreme of their peripheral vision to map the total extent of the seeing area. Here we found a definite contraction of the field of vision. The degree of contraction correlated with the fitness of the player. If the player was in top form with good aerobic ability, there was virtually no change in the field of vision. A person who played tennis once a week and didn't augment this once-a-week exercise program with running, walking, or swimming showed a progressive contraction of the field. Our findings were evident after one set and startling after three sets. The loss of twenty to thirty degrees of vision was common. Men and women were affected equally. However, except for the doubles game, peripheral vision is not needed.

Eye movement was also within normal limits. The tired player couldn't focus as well, but this would not affect his game as near vision is not important in tennis. Convergence, the mechanism by which both eyes turn in, as in the act of reading, was a little remote in the bushed player.

The most interesting findings came from the static field studies. A static field measures the light threshold of the retina, the area of the eye that receives the sensory impulses and sends them to the brain. With fatigue, there was a drop in sensitivity to light. The drop was not enough to create loss of field but enough to cause a shadow effect. Certainly the loss of light threshold was sufficient to reduce contrast. As contrast is important in maintaining dynamic acuity, it became apparent that this was the major cause of seeing the ball late.

We used the same monitor which tests the speed of a ball in flight to detect reaction time. With the serve and the net shots this lateness in detection of the ball was evident. There was no doubt that the zone of fog which normally surrounds impact was enlarged with fatigue. We did this study to differentiate motor or muscular fatigue from sensory or visual weariness. The players who were tired often couldn't reach the ball with one foot stationary and the racquet in readiness. So their muscular fatigue compounded their visual problem. They were unable to get to the ball except by reaching and running. This meant further deterioration of their vision as running creates visual loss of fine definition on its own. So they were late for the shot, unable to prepare for the shot with a proper foreswing, and were hitting the ball with minimal visual guidance. Typically, the shots were misdirected or were weak. Errors were common as the ball would strike the net or long shots would fall out of bounds. Most players noted a loss of consistency. Where they were making points by inches, now they were losing by inches.

With some players, there was no change in visual status or their dynamic acuity. They merely became tired in the ordinary way with inability to run, becoming winded and weary. Their aerobic reserves were obviously depleted.

It was surprising that some players could reach the ball but suffered from sensory fatigue as revealed in our static light threshold field studies. This kind of player who tired easily could improve his stroking by moving forward into the ball out of the zone of fog. But the weary tennis player doesn't move this way. He is generally unprepared for the shot and compounds his error by hitting the ball at his side rather in front of his body. On fast serves, the decay in sensory alertness was most apparent. These players could return the serve from twenty-five to fifty percent better in the first set as opposed to the third set.

There were no sexual differences with regard to sensory decay. Women were affected in the same way as men.

In most instances when a player said he lost his concentration or mental ability to perform well, it was generally due to a loss of motor or visual function. Such a player becomes discouraged by missing balls he knows he should retrieve and becomes resigned to losing. It doesn't take more than a few poorly played games before the player becomes dejected and ceases to entertain any hope of winning. The effort or thrust just is not there. At this point, the player does not expect to win, loses his desire, and of course loses his match.

Sensory fatigue is common. Many players are tigers in the warmup and in the first set. Aerobic fitness, then, separates the hobby tennis player from the athlete. The athlete just doesn't fatigue.

Borg, who may turn out to be the finest tennis player of all time, never seems to wane. John McEnroe who, like the rest of the tennis community, has difficulty bearing down on Borg says, "He is in the best shape of anyone. He is thin and he can run all day. Some guys you see panting. You never see Borg do that. You never know if he is tired."

Borg's aerobics are phenomenal. At age eighteen, tests at a Swedish sports medicine clinic revealed his resting heart rate to be thirty-eight beats per minute, while the average pulse beat is between seventy to eighty per minute. His fitness may also explain why Borg was able to keep his eye on the ball longer than other players as revealed in tournament photographs.

To avoid sensory deterioration in tennis, general fitness must be advocated as it compliments the well known beneficial effects of heart, lung, and muscular conditioning. Swimming, walking, jogging, and bicycle riding are all useful vehicles for attaining better conditioning. However, tennis players must play tennis. The visual side of the game is a mix of anticipation and vision. Without practice, the perfect mix will never occur. Besides illumination, the practice of trying to follow fast moving objects is the other major way of improving dynamic visual acuity. A great tennis player should be a good runner. He must be in shape to keep his performance level high and uniform over the duration of play.

A momentary rest between matches may be helpful, but has really superficial value. Rest is the obvious antidote to fatigue. But a player does not have the luxury of a long pause between matches. However, the game can be slowed down just simply by taking longer to retrieve balls and by having some blinking exercises between matches. With any concentrated activity, the blink rate goes drastically down be it reading or driving a car. In fact, the blink rate may drop from sixteen to twenty times per minute to four or five times. Fatigue often ensues when the eyes do not blink because of drying of the front surface of the eye, the cornea. Ten quick blinks may polish, hydrate, and generally refresh the eyes and is useful exercise for tired tennis players, weary, drivers, and glassy-eyed students. The same effect could be achieved with ordinary eye drops, collyria, but why bother with the cost and the inconvenience of eye drops when the most natural dropper is the lids and the best lubricant is your tears.

Visual fatigue is not subject to quick remedies. A combination of a general exercise program plus regular tennis is essential. Most players only practice baseline shots. They become adept at hitting slow low balls and eventually do it automatically. Sometimes they serve in a practice session but rarely do they attempt to practice a return of service, which is a crucial aspect of the game. The serve assumes huge importance because most players can't cope with speed. The eye's responsiveness is nurtured on slower shots and players often cannot convert slow tennis to the fast game. When a player becomes fatigued it is the fast game that goes first. A player will say that he "didn't see the ball" which is true. As the game presses on, a loss of contrast occurs. The ball is not seen distinctly — it is as though the lighting was reduced in intensity. A definite darkening effect occurs. The retinal, the sensory layer of the eye, loses its light sensitivity. Illumination is one of the keys to accurate visual timing or dynamic visual acuity. That is why it is best to see under conditions of outdoor tennis on a bright day. Essentially with fatigue one dims the lights from within. The best way to turn on those lights is by improving the aerobic capacity so that more oxygen can pass to the eye and brain.

● Eye injuries and precautions

Most tennis players do not wear eye protection. Indeed, it is not necessary for the majority of players to wear protection although the potential for a dangerous eye injury always exists. The following players are most prone to eye injury:

1) Players who frequently run to the net.
2) Those who play doubles.

3) Anyone who wears glasses that are not sufficiently strong to withstand the impact of a tennis ball.

4) Any player who has good vision in one eye only. This might apply to eight percent of the population as there are at least this many people with one lazy eye. With one eye alone the ability to discern depth and a ball in motion is poor. Protective glasses should be worn.

Volley shots at or near the net are most likely to cause an eye injury. The ball is fast and travels at eye level. McEnroe is not even looking at the ball.

The player who runs for the net and is set before his opponent makes the return is prepared to play the net and protect himself from the return. However, the player who is on the run may be struck by the ball because he is unable to see the return or he might not be completely set at the net. Tennis injuries as a rule are not common but when they happen, they invariably occur at the net.

The doubles player who concentrates on his game at the net plays dangerously. He is always intercepting the ball at its maximum velocity.

Oddly enough, a ball ricocheting from the player's own racquet is the second highest cause of tennis injuries. The deflection of the ball is too fast for reflex action. Again, because the velocity of the ball is greater in the forecourt, accidents of a more serious nature occur here.

Some tennis injuries have been reported during warm-ups, when more than one ball was in play on the same court. This is a dangerous situation because the eye can follow only one ball at a time. It is quite common to do this in doubles warm-ups where two players are at the net and two players are hitting from the back court with two balls going at the same time. This is quite a safe practice session as long as the opponents opposite each other can keep the ball on their own side of the court. However, in social tennis it is common for the men to play fast shots to one another while their wives play a slower game. (To avoid any misunderstanding, the same situation occurs with wives who are great players and whose husbands' erratic hitting sends tennis balls to the wrong side of the court.) At any rate, a player can see only one ball in motion and if another is accidently sent over he could be struck. The only redeeming feature of an eye injury is that the ball is larger than the eye so the impact is absorbed by the frontal bone above the eye, the malar bone below the eye, and the temporal bone to the side.

The type of tennis injuries that can occur to the face include lip lacerations, bruising of the lids of the eye, and hemorrhage of the eye. Cases of retinal tears, retinal detachment, and late developing cataracts and glaucoma have been reported. So the injuries may be serious and the consequences grave.

Contact lens wearers do not have any special jeopardy. If a tennis ball hits a soft lens, the effects of impact of the lens against the surface of the eye may create a minor abrasion but nothing serious. A hard lens is made of resilient plastic, so it will not shatter if struck. The surface abrasion may be more extensive but these usually heal without scarring or visual loss. However, contact lens wearers can suffer internal damage to the eye; so they require eye protection in high-risk areas.

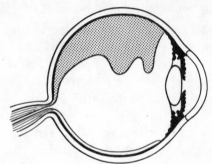

A detachment of the retina may result from the eye being struck by a tennis ball.

A

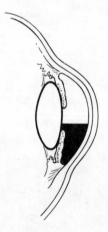

Haemorrhage occurring in the interior of the eye from contusion of the globe.

Occasionally freak accidents occur. We saw one player who was at the net, ready and prepared for the next shot. A bead of perspiration dropped into one eye, so he lowered his racquet to wipe his eye. At that moment, he was struck in the other eye by the tennis ball. Certainly anything can happen at the net and the best treatment is prevention.

● Safety precautions

People who normally wear glasses should get special safety glasses that are chemically or heat hardened and must be at least 3.0 mm thick to be able to withstand the impact of a one-inch steel ball dropped from a height of fifty inches. One should ask for 3.0 mm heat hardened lenses or plastic lenses specially designed to withstand the same tests. The best plastic is a polycarbonate which can withstand the impact of a bullet without shattering. Flexible nylon frames that have a cushioned rubber bridge are a good choice because the frames can be adjusted for comfort and will not snap if hit.

There are plastic guards available now, which can be used for tennis and squash, or racquet ball. These are made of shatterproof plastic and are transparent allowing the wearer wide peripheral vision. These protectors are form fitting, comfortable and completely protect the eye. The combat glasses are one of the best of these plastic guards.

Eye protection is now becoming commonplace. It has for years been mandatory in industry, and is now required for amateur hockey. Eye safety is actively promoted in squash and racquet ball, both of which have a high incidence of ocular injury.

Tennis is a little different. The ball is large and relatively soft, the racquet is large, and the proper ready position for a blocking shot is in front of the face. So a tennis racquet is a guard of sorts. Deflections from the net come up to the face without speed so there is little danger from a net-tipped deflection. Also, the orthopedic surgeons seem to command the greatest presence in this sport with endemic tennis elbows, torn knee ligaments and cartilages, and bad backs. The tensor bandage seems to be the bandaid of tennis.

Although eye injuries are not frequent, they tend to be serious when they occur. In high risk situations, always wear protective lenses.

● The fast ball as a threat

Although we consciously are not aware of any limitations to our vision, we react instinctively to an oncoming object travelling at a speed we cannot track. There is a certain amount of tension in dealing with balls that cannot be followed; at the net, such is the tension that we may raise our racquet over our face for self-protection rather than to play the net game.

The eyes will invariably close when threatened by a menacing stimulus. If there is a loud noise such as a clap of thunder, the eyes will close — this is called the *menace response*. If a hand reaches out toward the eyes in a quick and menacing manner, the lids will close. The same thing happens at the net in tennis. A fast ball is a visual threat. Many people, while playing the net, become very apprehensive when a fast ball comes at them. They respond by closing their eyes. It is self-protective gesture. They are not aware they are doing it, nor are they inconvenienced by the temporary loss of vision. The visual world remains whether the eyes are open or closed because one's visual memory takes over when the lights go out. It is somewhat like blinking — no one is aware of the off and on interruption of visual images which should occur when we blink. Yet we blink fifteen to twenty times per minute. If the lights in a room were actually turned off and on with the same frequency and duration of our blink response, the distraction would drive us crazy.

The degree of the menace response is quite variable. It can be a simple blink or more prolonged forceful lid closure. It is more prevalent in children and seems to be slightly more common in women than men. In tennis, it is certainly more common in beginners than among experienced players. In certain players, the forced lid closure can occur the moment that a ball is observed to be coming at them. The threatening gesture of a hard volley shot coming across may be sufficient to trigger the lids to close. The stimulus may be the windup for the shot rather than the approach of the ball itself. Like Pavlov's dog, the stimulus to threat may be sufficient to evoke a reaction. The threat of being injured is not imaginary or a neurotic obsession. Most injuries to the face and eyes occur during net play. Yet, despite the protective recess of the eye housed in a bony compartment, hemorrhages to the eye occur from contusion.

Of course it is not good tennis or a smart defensive reaction to play with closed eyes. The menace response is not a true reflex so it can be undone. Once a player learns to cope with speed of ball at the net, then the eyes will not feel threatened and forced lid closure will not follow. If you flick your fingers towards a friend's eyes at a dinner table he or she will invariably blink or close the eyes. If you do it repeatedly, blinking may occur the second or third time but eventually it will stop as the eyes cease to become alarmed by motion of the hand. The same is true in tennis. A player must be comfortable with speed not become anxious when confronted with fast tennis ball. It requires practice and net play to overcome this irritating non-productive visual habit. The key to comfortable net play is early anticipation. The racquet must be up, ready to block the moment the ball is struck by one's opponent. The ball may not be seen too clearly but the direction of the break in one's visual field can be accurately projected. It is like witnessing a flash of lightning. It may go off unexpectedly in your field of vision and you can accurately point or turn to its correct location. Early anticipation also provides the player with time to cover the ball. Once a player is not harassed by dangers of a fast tennis ball the eyes will not close. Video tapes of one's game may be very helpful on this matter because the player may or may not be aware of what their eyes and more particularly, their lids, are doing. You may not be able to follow a ball going at one hundred miles per hour but it certainly helps to keep your eyes open. The worst limitation you can place on your game is to keep your eyes closed because then your play is totally blind.

It is amazing in how many photographs we found players with their eyes closed when responding to volley shots at the net. These pictures were taken without a flash (a flash camera does evoke the menace response which is why so many flash pictures come out with the eyes closed). At first we threw out these pictures as they seemed to be just bad pictures. However, we eventually realized that the frequency of the eyes that were closed during net volleys was no accident. Eventually these players were repeatedly photographed after taking practice sessions with fast volley shots and finally could master the net game without the menace response. They became adjusted to speed and were not obliged to close their eyes at the approach of the ball.

 ## What to do in the event of injury

It is important to consult an eye doctor — an ophthamologist — to look after the medical consequences of an injury to the eye. Even if you feel no discomfort you may have a slight hemorrhage and not be aware of it. The blood may be absorbed but a few years down the road you could develop glaucoma or a cataract. Your pupil may be ruptured so that it remains semidilated and does not constrict to bright sun. Such a condition could be very troublesome for years to come.

If your eye is painful and it hurts to blink, you may have a traumatic ulcer on the surface of the eye. The lid must be immobilized to prevent it from constantly riding across the ulcerated surface. A firm patch over the closed lid should be applied.

We have treated the following injuries resulting from the impact of a tennis ball:

1) Hyphema: blood in the front chamber of the eye
2) Retinal Detachments: separation of the sensory layer of the eye
3) Subconjunctival Hemorrhage: bleeding in the filmy front surface membranes of the eye
4) Traumatic Ptosis: a lid droop
5) Corneal Ulcers
6) Late developing complications: glaucoma and cataracts
7) Skin abrasions and lacerations
8) Dislocation of the lens of the eye
9) Effects of contusion: swelling in the retina where precise vision occurs.

Do not put drops of any kind into the eye. Cover the injured eye with a clean, sterile gauze. The injured player should not be given anything to eat or drink, or pain-killing medication in the event surgery is required. Have the eye examined as soon as possible.

● Eye exercises to improve your tennis?

Visual calisthetics — sounds good. And there are programs to exercise the eyes. Unfortunately, they don't improve the strength of your eye muscles, improve your visual responses or help you to see better. You might as well eat carrots to help your tennis.

Eye muscles are unique in that they are the only voluntary muscles that are constantly at work and are continuously being exercised. So these muscles are normally working at full capacity and have maximum power. They cannot be made any stronger and even if they could there would be no point to it. If the eye could move faster vision would deteriorate during that rapid eye movement. Accurate vision occurs when the eyes are perfectly still or have paused after a rapid eye movement. The eyes can follow an object with reasonable clarity, but the object of regard has to move very slowly.

A good tennis player is like a good reader with respect to his eyes. A fast reader doesn't move his eyes any quicker than a slow reader. He merely takes few fixational pauses and the duration of these pauses are brief. A slow plodding reader will pause at every word. A child learning to read must pause from word to word and spend a great deal of time coping with each word. Every syllable of the word must be comprehended until vision and comprehension are simultaneous.

In tennis, the mechanism for following a ball travelling at great speed is with rapid eye movement. A player learning the game must start with the slow game. He must build up eye-hand coordination. He must have the visual security of seeing the ball close to impact. This is easily done just with lessons or play.

For the beginner, both the lessons and game are so slow that the function of the eye is not really challenged. The ball comes over the net lazily and the bounce can be seen. There is sufficient time to not only move the eyes but also to move the head along the flow of the ball. It is equivalent to reading "Dick and Jane" in grade one.

Once a player is swinging and can hit the ball across the net the tempo of the game increases. The velocity of the ball is still slow and can be regulated by merely waiting for the ball or stepping back to let the ball slow down. The path of the ball can be easily followed as it comes across the net. A shift in position of the eyes is only required when the ball is close in. At this point, which is usually near the bounce and depends upon the speed of the ball, the eye has to move. In the slow game, all a player has to do is make a fast motion of his eyes and pause and he will see the ball again. Remember, however, when the eyes are in motion vision is suppressed.

The ball has a regular course because at the beginner's level of play there will be no spins to sides or topspin rushes after the bounce. Therefore, the eyes have problem holding the pathway of the ball and taking in more visual information. The same visual device is used in reading except that the print isn't moving. Now a novice player or early intermediate may be able to make several visual stops before hitting the ball. He is very conscious of his eyes because some coach is screaming "Keep your eyes on the ball."

Once a player has hit intermediate status, his troubles begin. The first serve is no longer a puff ball. If he is playing someone of his own calibre, the hard serve — generally a flat serve — will fall in fifteen to twenty percent of the time. The player is confronted with baseline shots that have some muscle, even though more than half the shots go into the net or travel long. Visually it is a new game.

On the service that goes in, there is insufficient time to make numerous visual stops. The ball travels too fast to make many pauses along its course. Yet it is possible to see the ball relatively well with just a couple of visual stops. Some players adapt easily while others never go beyond this stage. Like a poor reader, they have juvenile visual patterns. They take in very little information per visual rest and require multiple stops.

Once a player is at this plateau, he can do two things. He can accept his lot and play social tennis or he can begin to learn to cope with speed. If the person wants to improve, he must do it on the tennis court. Other than racquet sports, there is no other place that a person in motion has to track an object in motion. So, it is not possible to do home calisthenics on the eyes. It must be done on the tennis court.

A ball machine is an excellent training partner. A player

doesn't have to run so that the only factor of importance is the increasing speed of the ball. Also a ball machine doesn't miss. By increasing the speed of the ball, you are forcing your eyes to do two things. Make fewer visual stops along the course of the ball and expand the information given at each pause so you know where the ball is going without looking at it constantly. You will also learn that one way to cut down on the visual flight pattern of the ball is to make it shorter. If you step into the ball and hit it early, you are actually cutting short the amount of visual tracking. So you must begin to move forward into the ball and not be content to hit it at the side. It will also improve your stroke because the arc of the foreswing will be longer so there will be more power in the shot. An added bonus will be your consistency. As the stroke is full, the control of the ball will be greater. There is greater chance that the wrist will be firm when impact is made halfway along a full swing.

Once you feel you can answer a ball machine, then you have to apply your talents to the court. The big difference is running. Some players run too slow or don't move early enough so they have to hit in motion. A fast moving ball against a fast moving player produces a blurred event. You can't control the speed of the ball. You can control your own motion. Leave early for the next shot and try to arrive at the ball when the head, body, and eyes are not in motion. If your racquet is ready, and you move into the shot you have a reasonably good chance of hitting the ball properly.

You have done three things: placed the eyes in a stop position; cut the length of the course of the ball; and eliminated the vertical ups and downs of running.

Some players never get beyond this stage. They hit the ball beautifully provided they're at center court within three feet of the baseline. Once they meet a player who can move them, their game falls apart.

How do you practice playing against increasing motion and speed on the ball? You must challenge better players constantly until you find the level of your playing competence. Eventually, you will find an end point to your ability which is governed by your fitness, coordination, your visual prowess, and your determination. But the only way to improve your eye is to play regularly and with faster players.

Eventually, a player can progress to the point where there are no visual stops. The speed of the ball is so fast that a player is fortunate to reach the ball with one foot on the ground even with good anticipation and swift running. He usually encounters this kind of action on return of service hit by an advanced player. If a ball is coming at great speeds, you will only see it coming across the net. Once it moves into the bounce area it is lost. The good player will make zero visual stops and will not attempt to follow the ball. The eyes will be straight, the head straight, and the player's orientation not even directed to the ball. The zone of fog is large and thick and the player looks to the last place he saw the ball clearly.

There are no artificial eye exercises to help cope with this situation. The best exercise is a good game of tennis or playing the fast segment of game on a practice court with a coach or a professional.

You should remember the following points:

1) As the ball goes faster, your contact with the ball must be more forward in front of the body. On a return of service, frequently a chip shot or frontal blocking motion is the best that can be done.
2) You may not see the ball, but you must act on the visual slips of information available like a fast reader scanning a page.
3) Do not try and keep your eye on a fast ball. Play the motion, not the ball.
4) The faster the ball, the quicker you must be to get to the ball to make the most accurate visual assessment. It is best that the total motion of the body be stopped.
5) With fatigue, you will extend the length and density of the zone of fog.
6) The best visual exercise for a game of tennis is a game of tennis . It is the only way to build up your dynamic visual acuity.
7) Practice velocity warm-ups. Add to your practice session return of serves as well as serves.

The "Catch 22" of the eye game is that it is not really possible to voluntarily control your eyes and force them to set in a particular position. As you read this page, do you know where your eyes are or are you aware that they are darting in a jerk-like fashion across the page? Can you feel the jerky, fast motions of your eyes?

There is no voluntary positional sense. The players we tested who thought they kept their eyes on the ball, did not. They were unaware that their eyes were straight ahead when the ball was at their racquet. Only when we showed them their own photograph did they accept the information.

Jimmy Connors: His eyes and head are not directed toward the ball.

A player can try to follow the ball into the racquet, but has no physiological device that can determine whether this is actually being accomplished. He can, however, follow a slow moving object. Just pass a pencil through your field of vision and you will see it and know that your eyes are moving transversely in unison with the motion of the pencil.

In the fast game of tennis there is no conscious awareness of the eyes. In fact, much of our body movement is quite automatic and rhythmic. We can consciously learn a stroke, dissect it to its component parts, bring together again, but when we do it in a game we are not aware of it. With the eyes, the only way to control their action is to be aware of their abilities and limitations. A player should know the visual importance of head and eye stability before stroking. A player can move forward into a fast ball. The eyes will respond appropriately. A player should be prepared for fast action as soon as his opponent signals his intent because he may not see the ball and requires a mix of anticipation and readiness to hit the ball properly. A player should accept the insecurity of blind shots like the return of service and the half volley which may be in a fog zone before the bounce. Most important, as the player develops tennis skills, he cannot apply slow game techniques to fast tennis. Both the body and visual dynamics are quite different from one another.

The "Catch 22" of tennis is that we cannot recommend abstract eye exercises. The only exercise that is valid, as we have mentioned before, is that acquired through a game of tennis.

10 Basic Rules to Improve Your Game

1) Start quickly for each shot and run as slowly as possible to meet the ball. Despite the apparent paradox here, the player should try and reach the ball with at least one foot stable to ensure best visual stability and power. With the body in motion, vision is poor. Also, while running there is no body stability to leverage a shot. So it is sensible to advocate a fast start.

Running as slowly as possible is recommended because running spoils a player's tracking ability of the eye. The faster the run, the worse the vision. Good players seem to glide. They run with a smooth motion. The choppy up-and-down movement of a sprinter with bursts of acceleration will sharply reduce visual acuity. The purpose of the fast start is to enable you to slow down your lateral runs.

Also the faster you run, the poorer will be your visual spacing. You will either run into the ball or reach for it and hit the ball at the distal side of the sweet spot.

The worst performance will be delivered by the player who waits until the ball is in motion and then has to scurry to meet the ball. That player may be only a half step out of proper approach to the ball but will not be able to put any real power into the shot. You have to be on the ground to deliver maximum power and control to a shot. It can't be done while stretched out or with the elbow parked in the navel.

2) Tailor your shot to the speed of the ball. The faster the ball is travelling, the more imperative it is to hit in front of the body. The player who delays and allows his game to

become automatic with reference to a slow moving ball will never be able to improve. His motions are frozen and his approach to the ball the same whether the ball is at zero velocity and ready to drop or is at a great speed. Visually it is a disaster to try and follow the faster balls into the racquet. Anticipate early and move into the trajectory of the ball.

Many club players experience no growth or maturity in their tennis development because their game is too rigid. Their motor memory is catered to the slow game. Such players will do a little better playing on clay or slow synthetics. If you can't convert your game and your visual habit is too ingrained in following the ball, the next best thing is to slow down the game itself, by hitting lobs and medium-paced shots to the baseline.

3) A large racquet with an enlarged sweet spot will offer advantages to the player who is slow, unfit, too lazy to run and too preoccupied to anticipate. The visual deterioration inherent in a moving game is compensated by increasing the size of the target. If a tennis racquet were the size of a baseball bat the game would be unplayable.

The larger racquet does debilitate some shots while assisting others. The racquet is more awkward to manipulate especially for players who add wrist to their shot. There is nothing wrong with being a wristy player as Tom Okker of the Netherlands or Rod Laver of Australia have shown, but choose a smaller racquet. If your game is predicated on the serve and scamper-to-the-net-type of game, you won't like playing with the bottom of a basket. The power of the service is derived from a snap of the wrist and the big racquet won't come down as well. The aerodynamics of a large and small racquet may be the same but in clinical tests of the big racquet, most players who sampled the jumbo machine found it lacking in manoeuvrability.

The large racquet is wonderful for doubles, especially mixed doubles. Women who play with their husbands in social tennis often have to cope with faster play, so they can't see a fast ball nor can they respond to it. This problem is augmented in doubles because the net game is paramount and the volley shot is king. A volley shot is one of the fastest in tennis as the energy of the ball is not dissipated by the bounce, so a bigger racquet compensates for the visual loss.

4) Anticipation is the antidote to the blurred vision of a fast game. A player who doesn't anticipate simply avoids the fast shots of the game. He doesn't go near the net and backs away from the service by playing far behind the baseline especially for the first serve. By avoiding the net, a player misses some of the excitement of the game. By moving back to convert a fast ball into a slow one adds to your displacement from the ball. Simply, you have to run much farther laterally, the more you drop back. So whatever visual gains you make by hitting a slower ball you lose by having to run farther and faster.

5) Look before you serve. Your eyes are focused on the ball and not on your opponent's service court. In other words you are hitting quite blind. Your arm does the seeing. Players who play the game daily or several times a week develop excellent motor memory. Hitting the service court becomes as automatic as scratching behind your ear. The sensory mechanism is proprioception or position sense of the limbs based on sensory receptors in muscles and joints which reveal our body position. Unless you are a total tennis machine like Borg, some visual augmentation is helpful. Look at the service court, etch in your mind where you wish to serve, and direct your shot to that place which only exists in your visual memory.

It is easy to become distracted. If you throw the ball too high, you will only think of hitting the ball on its descent. The ball should be tossed about three feet so at its apex of ascent, the outstretched body and racquet strikes the ball centrally. Errors in the ball toss — too high, too low, too far back, too far forward — are the prime result of distraction. Learn how to toss the ball like a machine so that all you have to think about is your opponent's service court etched in your mind.

6) If your depth perception is poor, avoid the net game and volley shots and let your lobs bounce. How do you know if your depth perception is off? Look at a sign, a clock, a television set or any visual target further away than ten feet and determine if you can see it clearly with each eye. If your vision is poorer in one eye, assume your depth perception is not precise. Depth perception requires the coordinated use of the two eyes seeing together. One good eye can't do the job of two eyes.

The lob shot is hard to assess moving in space. For body position trace the ball with your free hand so at least your place is under the dropping ball. Keep your eye on the ball as it falls and your racquet ready as if you were going to serve — in the back scratch position. Remember the ball is dropping quickly whereas in a service hit, the ball is struck just before it falls at almost zero velocity. If a smash is intended you must hit the ball earlier and higher than if a slower moving place shot is wanted. The speed of the racquet determines the visual complexity of the shot. A smash is more difficult because a moving ball is met by a fast racquet and the area of impact is enveloped in a dense fog. If the ball is hit more slowly, then the visual hold on the ball is longer and the shot is apt to be more precise. Concentrate on placing the overhead smash; develop accuracy and gradually add the power. If your depth perception is wanting, allow the ball to bounce. Another way out is to avoid rushing the net, and miss the lob scene completely.

7) The only person who can judge with reasonable accuracy whether a ball is in or out is a net man who is perfectly still. A moving player is a poor judge because he is a handicapped eyewitness. So nobody playing a singles game should become uptight about line calls. If you set angry during play because of a call against you, remember that your calls will probably be just as bad as your opponent's.

If your depth perception is poor, your judgement will be worse than normal which, as we have said, is not too precise.

If you wear glasses to play tennis, forget about the accuracy of your eyes. The movement of your glasses on your nose will cause parallax as you run. This displacement of the spectacles, frames and lenses will create a prismatic image jump. A near-sighted person will see the ball smaller and the jump will be "with" the motion of the glasses.

If the glasses move up, the ball will be displaced upwards. A far-sighted person wearing glasses will see the ball larger and it will appear to move opposite the movement of the glasses. So anybody wearing glasses will not get an accurate picture of the object — the tennis ball moving in space.

The best judge in tennis is the player who will realize the fallability of his visual perceptions and either award the points to his opponent or ask for a reply of the point. The worst scene occurs when a courteous player meets a visual jock who insists he can see the seams of the ball on a return of serve. Avoid making the game a frustrating experience. After all, tennis is a game and it should be a tension release and not an aggravating experience.

In professional tennis, the player who insists on making his own line calls deserves the derision he receives from the audience, the critics and the media.

8) The net game should be an integral part of every warm-up to avoid the menace response. The menace response is simply an automatic lid closure to any stimulus that threatens the eye. In a tennis game, a fast ball at the net definitely threatens the eye. So many players close their eyes when they see a tennis ball coming their way. The lid closure is involuntary and prolonged — it is not a blink. The player is not aware that he does it.

The only way this reaction can be controlled is the practice volley shots at the net. Once the eyes are not threatened or intimidated by the ball, they will stay open. Once a player feels comfortable at the net, he can once again use his racquet as intended — to play tennis rather than as a facial protector.

9) Be aware of the symptoms of sensory fatigue. The most common symptoms are listed below.

— You are late in seeing the ball. There does not seem to

be enough time to get the racquet back to make a full swing.

— You lose your concentration. It is difficult to follow the ball and, without knowing it, you move back to take the ball slower.

— You complain about the lighting. It seems darker and of course you lose dynamic visual acuity which requires contrast.

— You begin to make gross errors at line calls. Balls that land a foot in or out are called incorrectly.

— You decrease the frequency of volly shots and are less inclined to head for the net.

— You begin to have difficulty with return of service shots. You become victim of high bounces off topspin shots and slice returns. You do not anticipate correctly because you do not see your opponent as clearly as before.

— You have to run faster because you don't estimate the speed of the ball correctly. Sensory fatigue is a prelude to a more demanding running game. You start to miss even the occasional ball because you can't reach it.

— You are only competitive in the first thirty minutes of singles play and then your game goes off.

What to do about it? Aerobic fitness is the key. The eyes are merely a camera taking pictures which are then relayed to the occipital cortex, the visual area of the brain. When the oxygen supply to the brain is off, the light sensitivity of the brain is depressed. There is a definite darkening effect.

A good tennis player should be a good athlete. The aerobic game is well known. Running, walking, swimming, or bicycling on a regular basis is essential to promote endurance in strenuous games like tennis.

There are no magic drops for tired eyes. Even if these were, it would be a hoax, because the act of seeing is a cerebral function.

Eye exercises are a waste of time. Visual judgement can be enhanced, but the best exercise for promoting dynamic visual acuity in a game of tennis is to play tennis.

There is no doubt, that in the players we tested, sensory fatigue was earlier and more profound among the weekend club players who thought they were getting into shape than the players who played tennis for sport and did other things to keep in shape.

10) Getting to the net after a serve. Ideally, you should glide with long strides and follow the direction of your serve. The center of the net should not be an objective. The return of your service must be directed at a low angle or in the same direction of your original serve. The latter is especially apt to happen if your opponent merely blocks the serve using the power of your service for his own return.

11) One of the most difficult shots to make from a visual point of view is the half volley. It is totally a blind hit. Even the bounce is not seen. The ratio of anticipation to vision is 100% anticipation and zero vision. The half volley is a forced stroke executed when a ball is aimed at your feet or during a rush to the net when a volley shot can't be made.

It is a stay-alive shot because it has neither power or placement. The racquet must be open-faced to force the ball to clear the net and the player must get down on the ball so that the return won't be an easy lob for the opponent player.

12) Of all the coaching clichés, the one that is most apt to make trouble is "Keep Your Eye on the Ball." It is not possible nor desirable, nor is it necessary. In fact — *it could ruin your tennis.*

BIBLIOGRAPHY

Beals, R.P.; Mayyasi, A.M.; Templeton, A.E.; Johnston, W.L. "The Relationship between Basketball Shooting Performance and Certain Visual Attributes." *American Journal of Optometry and Archives of American Academy of Optometry,* July 1971.

Brody, Howard. "The Physics of the Tennis Racquet." *American Journal of Physics* 47 (1979): 482-87.

Brown, Brian. "Dynamic Visual Acuity, Eye Movements, and Peripheral Acuity for Moving Targets." *Vision Research* 12: 305-21.

Brown, Brian. "The Effect of Target Contrast Variation on Dynamic Visual Acuity and Eye Movements." *Vision Research* 12: 1213-24.

Brown, Brian; Adams, Anthony J.; Haegerstrom-Portney, G.; Jones, R.T.; Flom, M.C. "Effects of Alcohol and Marijuana on Dynamic Visual Acuity — Threshold Measurements." *Perception and Psychophysics* 18 (1975): 441-46.

Burg, Albert. "Vision and Driving : A Report on Research." *Human Factors* 13 (1971): 79-87.

Burg, Albert. "Apparatus for Measurement of Dynamic Visual Acuity." *Perceptual and Motor Skills* 20 (1965): 231-34.

Burg, Albert. "Visual Acuity as Measured by Dynamic and Static Tests — A Comparative Evaluation." *Journal of Applied Psychology* 50, no. 6 (1966), pp. 460-66.

Colenbrander, M.C. "Visual Acuity, Visual Field, and Physical Ability." Netherlands Ophthalmology Society, 166th Meeting, Eindhoven 1971.

Committee on Medical Aspects of Automotive Safety. "Visual Factors in Automobile Driving." *Archives of Ophthalmology* 81 (1969).

Committee on Medical Aspects of Automobile Safety. "Medical Aspects of Driver Limitation." *The Journal of the American Medical Association* 187 (1964): 376.

Deshaies, Paul, and Pargman, David. "Selected Visual Abilities of College Football Players." *Perceptual and Motor Skills* 43 (1976): 904-06.

Feldhaus, J.L. Jr. "Dynamic Visual Acuity — Effect on Night Driving and Highway Driving." *Highway Research Board Bulletin,* no. 298.

Gabbard, Carl P., and Shea, Charles H. "Influence of Movement Activities on Shape Recognition and Retention." *Perceptual and Motor Skills* 48 (1979): 116-18.

Garner, A.I., O.D. "An Overlooked Problem: Athletes' Visual Needs." *The Physician and Sportsmedicine* 5, no. 4, 1977.

Getz, Donald J., O.D., F.A.A.O., F.C.O.V.D. "Vision and Sports." *Journal of American Optometric Association* 49, no. 4 (1978).

Gregory, R.L. *Eye and Brain — The Psychology of Seeing.* New York: McGraw-Hill Book Co., 1966.

Harrison, William, and Mitchell, Matt. "Target Your Thoughts." *Golf Magazine,* June 1978.

Henderson, R.L., and Burg, A. "Driver Screening for Night Driving." *Highway Research Board,* no. 156.

Hilbourne, J.F.H. "Social and Other Aspects of Adjustments to Single Eye Cataract Extraction in Elderly Patients." *Trans. Ophthalomology Society,* U.K. (1975): 95, 254.

Keeney, Arthur H., M.D. "Ophthalmic Pathology in Driver Limitation." *American Academy of Ophthalmology and Otolaryngology,* September-October 1968.

Keeney, Arthur H. "Assessment of Special Visual Function." In *The Assessment of Visual Function* edited by A.M. Potts. St. Louis: C.V. Mosby Co., 1972.

Kochhar, D.S., and Fraser, T.M. "Monocular Peripheral Vision as a Factor in Flight Safety." *Aviation, Space, and Environmental Medicine,* May 1978.

Miller, James W., Ph.D., and Ludvigh, Elek, Ph.D. "The Effect of Relative Motion on Visual Acuity." *Survey of Ophthalmology.*

Morehouse, Chauncey A., Ph.D.; Krecklow, Douglas E., B.Sc.; Fisher, John T., M.D.; Welling, Thomas W.; Morrison, William E., M.Sc. "Soft Contact Lenses for Sports." *The Physician and Sportsmedicine,* May 1978.

Myers, Kenneth J., Ph.D., O.D. "Marathon Running and Vision." *Journal of the American Optometric Association* 47, no. 4 (1967).

Nelson, J.I. "Motion Sensitivity in Peripheral Vision." *Perception,* vol. 3 (1974), pp. 151-51.

Personal Communication — Brian Brown, Ph.D., Smith Kettlewell Institute of Visual Sciences, University of The Pacific, San Francisco.

Personal Communication — Albert Burg, Ph.D., Human Factors Safety Specialist, Los Angeles, California

Personal Communication — Arthur Keeney, Dean, School of Medicine, University of Louisville, Louisville, Kentucky.

Personal Communication — William Harrison, Vision Dynamics, Laguna Beach, California.

Petrakis, Elizabeth. "Perceptual Style of Varsity Tennis Players." *Perceptual and Motor Skills* 48 (1979): 266.

Salmela, John H., and Fiorito, Pierre. "Visual Clues in Ice Hockey Goaltending." *Canadian Journal of Applied Sport Science,* vol. 4, no. 1, (1979), pp. 56-59.

Slatt, B., and Stein, H.A. "Eye Protectors." *Racquets Canada,* April 1979.

Stein, H.A., and Slatt, B. *Fitting Guide for Hard and Soft Contact Lenses.* St. Louis: C.V. Mosby Co., 1977.

Stein, H.A., and Slatt B. *Introductory Manual for the Ophthalmic Assistant.* St. Louis: C.V. Mosby Co., 1976.

Stein, H.A., and Slatt B. *Why Wear Glasses if You Want Contacts?* New York: Simon and Schuster, 1976.

Stein, H.A., and Slatt, B., *The Ophthalmic Assistant.* 3rd. ed. St. Louis: C.V. Mosby Co., 1976.

Stein, H.A., and Slatt, B. "Swimming and Soft Contact Lenses." *Contact and Intraocular Lens Medical Journal* 3, no. 3, (1977).

Stein, H.A., and Slatt, B. "Important News Advances in Contact Lenses." *Health Magazine,* winter (1977).

Stein, H.A., and Slatt, B. "Complications of Prolonged Wear Hydrogel Lenses." *Contact and Intraocular Lens Medical Journal* 5, no. 1 (1979), p. 82.